D0376248

If *my* Heart Could Talk

If *my* Heart Could Talk

A Story of Family, Faith, and Miracles

Dodie Osteen
Foreword by Joel Osteen

FaithWords

New York   Boston   Nashville

Copyright © 2016 by Dodie Osteen
Cover design by Jerry Cooley
Cover and author photograph by Eric Forsythe
Cover copyright © 2017 by Hachette Book Group, Inc.

All rights reserved. In accordance with the U.S. Copyright Act of 1976, the scanning, uploading, and electronic sharing of any part of this book without the permission of the publisher constitute unlawful piracy and theft of the author's intellectual property. If you would like to use material from the book (other than for review purposes), prior written permission must be obtained by contacting the publisher at permissions@hbgusa.com. Thank you for your support of the author's rights.

FaithWords
Hachette Book Group
1290 Avenue of the Americas
New York, NY 10104
faithwords.com
twitter.com/faithwords

First Trade Paperback Edition: April 2017
FaithWords is a division of Hachette Book Group, Inc.
The FaithWords name and logo are trademarks of Hachette Book Group, Inc.

The publisher is not responsible for websites (or their content) that are not owned by the publisher.

The Hachette Speakers Bureau provides a wide range of authors for speaking events. To fin d out more, go to www.hachettespeakersbureau.com or call (866) 376-6591.

Unless otherwise indicated, all Scripture quotations are taken from the *New King James Version* of the Bible. Copyright © 1982 by Thomas Nelson, Inc. Used by permission. All rights reserved.

Scripture quotations noted NLT are taken from the *Holy Bible, New Living Translation*, copyright © 1996, 2004, 2007 by Tyndale House Foundation. Used by permission of Tyndale House Publishers, Inc., Carol Stream, Illinois 60188. All rights reserved.

Scripture quotations noted AMP are from the *Amplifi ed Bible*. Copyright © 2015 by The Lockman Foundation, La Habra, CA 90631. All rights reserved.

Scripture quotations noted NIV are taken from *The Holy Bible: New International Version*® NIV®. Copyright © 1973, 1978, 1984, 2011 by Biblica, Inc.™ Used by permission. All rights reserved worldwide.

All Scriptures marked NASB are from the *New American Standard Bible*®, copyright © 1960, 1962, 1963, 1968, 1971, 1972, 1973, 1975, 1977, 1995 by The Lockman Foundation. Used by permission.

Scriptures noted ESV are taken from the *The Holy Bible: English Standard Version*®, copyright © 2001 by Crossway, a publishing ministry of Good News Publishers. All rights reserved. Used by permission.

Scripture noted NCV are taken from the New Century Version®. Copyright © 2005 by Thomas Nelson. Used by permission. All rights reserved.

Library of Congress Cataloging-in-Publication Data has been applied for

ISBNs: 978-1-4555-4975-7 (trade paperback)

This book is dedicated to my beloved husband of forty-four-plus years, John Osteen. He was a kind and gentle man, full of compassion and love for me and everyone. A great teacher of the Word of God and a lover of all people, he saw no difference in color, nationality, rich or poor. John taught me how to be a pastor's wife when I didn't know where to begin, overlooking my mistakes. He was such a good father and shepherd of his flock. He was quick to obey God and he was real. I loved him and am so glad he asked me to be his bride in 1954. I think he would like my book!

Contents

Foreword   ix

Chapter 1:   This Pilgrim Made Progress   1

Chapter 2:   You Walk Like a Princess   14

Chapter 3:   A Legacy of Faith   27

Chapter 4:   Touch of the Master's Hand   37

Chapter 5:   Marrying My Pastor   49

Chapter 6:   Keep the Laughter in Your Marriage   57

Chapter 7:   Our First Miracle   70

Chapter 8:   Beginning to Fly   82

Chapter 9:   From a Feed Store to Feeding Millions   91

Chapter 10:   A Mother's Prayer   104

Chapter 11:   Healed of Cancer   116

Chapter 12:   Christmas Memories   130

Chapter 13:   The Gray Box   140

Chapter 14:   God's Got You Covered   152

Chapter 15:   Freedom Is Yours   163

Chapter 16:   Flying over Fear   172

Chapter 17:   Miracles behind "The Miracle"   180

Chapter 18:   Lessons from a Man's Best Friend   189

Chapter 19:   44 Years, 4 Months, and 6 Days   195

Chapter 20:   Filling John's Shoes   206

Chapter 21: God's Face Is Turned toward You 217

Chapter 22: Who Are You Running For? 226

Chapter 23: Moments of Mercy 236

Conclusion 245

Appendix 1: The Plan of Salvation 249

Appendix 2: Scriptural Confessions 251

Appendix 3: Healing Scriptures 253

Acknowledgments 269

Foreword by Joel Osteen

I may be a little biased, but I truly believe that my mother is the most amazing mother in the world. Her love, kindness, generosity, and strength of faith have inspired not only me but also countless others around the world. I love her dearly and feel honored to call her my mother.

When I was growing up, my mother ran a household with five very active children, a husband, a dog and countless other pets, cooked, cleaned, did endless piles of laundry and stacks of dishes . . . and she somehow made it look easy. Oh, and there was also helping with a fast-growing church that had hundreds of needs to be met. She seemed to never run out of energy, and she had a way of always making things fun along the way.

I don't recall ever leaving for school in the morning without my mother praying over me. And it wasn't just a "God bless the children" prayer. She would pray a hedge of protection around me and confidently speak God's favor over my life and that I would excel in every way. I wish that every child going to school today could feel what it means to know that God is going with them to school as I did.

That is just who my mother is—a woman of faith whose life and ministry were shaped through adversity and great challenges. As you read this book, you'll see exactly what I mean, and I have no doubt that you'll be inspired by her message.

The beauty of my mother's life is that she is a woman of great integrity. For me, that means she is the same at home as she is in the church and whenever she is in front of other people. She isn't perfect, and she's never pretended to be. But there has never been a double standard with Mother. Her sincerity has had a tremendous impact on me and my siblings, and I'm sure it's a significant reason why today all five of us are working in the ministry.

Mother is a constant source of inspiration to us.

I think of how my mother refused to be a victim when, as a young girl, she developed the dreaded disease of polio and had to wear a heavy brace on her leg for many years. She could have easily said, "God, this isn't fair. Why did this happen to me?" But she saw herself as the victor, and God brought her out of that difficulty.

When my mother was diagnosed with terminal cancer back in 1981, she could easily have come home and just sunk into a deep pit of depression. I'll never forget what a shock that news was to our family. But my mother never gave up. She refused to speak words of defeat. She didn't complain about how sick or weak she felt or how hopeless her situation looked. No, she chose to put God's words in her mind and in her mouth. All during the day, we'd hear Mother going through the house speaking aloud, "I shall not die but live, and declare the works of the Lord" from Psalm 118. I'd say, "Mother, how are you doing?" She'd say, "Joel, I'm strong in the Lord and the power of His might." As Mother mixed her words with God's words, something powerful began to happen, and as you'll read, she received her amazing healing. Mother remains cancer-free, healed by the power of God and His Word!

There's so much I could tell you about my mother. I could tell you about how much she loved and adored my father. No matter what Daddy faced through the years, he always knew that she was for him one hundred percent, and to Daddy that was all that really mattered. They were a team, and what they accomplished, they accomplished together. Growing up, I saw that and felt that and it impacted me profoundly.

And when Daddy departed this life and went to Heaven, Mother didn't fade away and go sit at home. In a time of profound loss and sadness, she realized that God still had great things in store for her, and she has soared in a God-sized way. It has been awesome to watch. I know that Daddy is smiling, and so am I.

There is a lot of my mother's life, example, and wisdom in this book. The lessons she taught me have changed my life, and these simple truths can change your life as well.

Joel Osteen

If *my* Heart Could Talk

Chapter 1

This Pilgrim Made Progress

The steps of a *good* man are ordered by the
Lord.

Psalm 37:23

Pelly, Texas. You've probably never heard of it, but that's
where I was born on October 22, 1933. You don't have to
do the math; I am eighty-two years young at the time of this
writing and still going strong. I never plan to retire! I have
too much to do for Jesus.

Dolores Ann Pilgrim is what my sweet parents named
me. For many years my nickname was Pooky, but eventually
Dodie became the nickname that stuck. Over the years, people have often referred to me as Pastor John Osteen's wife.
He was the founder of Lakewood Church in Houston, Texas,
and a remarkable husband, father, and man of God. Now

many refer to me as Joel Osteen's mother! But I'm just Dodie, a lady who loves God and people and a mother of five wonderful children who all happen to be in the full-time ministry. I hope that as I share bits of my story with you, you will be encouraged and blessed.

So back to my little town. Pelly was a town about thirty-seven miles east of Houston near the Goose Creek Oil Field. It was the home of the Humble Oil and Refining Company, which is now one of the largest ExxonMobil refineries in the world. In 1948, Pelly was renamed Baytown because it is located on the mouth of the San Jacinto River on Galveston Bay. I guess that's why I always loved being around water and the beach.

I was the only child born to Roy and Georgia Pilgrim, the best parents a daughter could ever wish for. They were good people. Good in the sense that they loved God, took me to church on Sundays, and showered me with love. But they were also good *to* people and went out of their way to lend a helping hand and to simply bless others. It was not unusual for Daddy to mow a neighbor's lawn just to help them out or for Mother to bake one of her delicious cherry pies or German chocolate cakes for friends, neighbors, or church members. They lived a good life, but it wasn't without overcoming some of life's greatest challenges.

Daddy was born in 1905 in the small town of Pine in central Texas as one of five children. There were four boys and one girl. He was only four years old when tragedy struck his family for the first time. It was around Christmastime, and Daddy and his brother were playing with firecrackers when one of the firecrackers landed on the roof and caught the house on fire. His mother ran out of the house with their tiny four-day-old baby brother. She had not yet recovered from the delivery, and as she ran she stumbled and fell and began to bleed profusely. Daddy said he vividly remembers his mother running fast, leaving a trail of blood behind her the whole way. Eventually she hemorrhaged to death. What a blow it was to the family!

Granddaddy Pilgrim did his best to work hard and take care of the children, but three years later tragedy struck a second time when he went to Scott and White Hospital in Tyler, Texas, thinking he was going to have a hernia repaired. He was a logger who worked hard lifting heavy logs all day. As he was being driven to the hospital in a horse and buggy, he said something no one ever forgot: "They will bring my body back home in a box." Those words came true. I guess Granddaddy had a sense that he was not going to live long.

My daddy told the story of how he rode home in the buggy that carried his father's casket to Willow Oak Cemetery— the creaking of the buggy and the wooden box that carried the shattered hopes and dreams of his family. What a tall order for such a young boy.

So by the time Daddy was only seven years old, he and his siblings were orphans. They needed parents, and they deserved good ones. Relatives came in and divided the children up, taking them into their homes. The children were separated, but at least they had someplace to call home and someone to call family.

Daddy didn't have an easy life and was treated badly. He had to sleep in the barn and wasn't allowed to attend school past junior high because he was required to work in the fields. His pay was only about fifty cents a week, and at Christmastime he would only get a quarter and an orange. Daddy may have only had an eighth-grade education, but he was always smart in my book. At eighteen years old, he packed his bags and started out on his own. At first he got a job building bridges with the railroad, but later he moved to Pelly and began working in the refineries of Humble Oil. He endured the heat, the heavy physical toil, and the toll both took, but he didn't complain; despite the hardships, he was never a victim.

My daddy was a slender, handsome man, part American Indian, who stood five feet eleven inches tall. Soon after settling in Pelly, he met my mother, Georgia Lee Case, a beautiful young woman who grew up there. Mother was the oldest of six children and a true Southern lady. She never met a stranger. To her, everyone was "Honey," "Darling," or "Sweetheart." Mother's daddy worked for Gulf Oil, and they lived in a pretty little house on the water. She and Daddy started dating soon after they met.

Mother made Daddy very happy, and her family adored him. They got married on August 4, 1928, and spent their honeymoon on Galveston Island. I have a picture of them taken on the beach in front of a famous restaurant in the background. I took the picture to show the owner and his family wanted a copy. It still hangs in the restaurant there on the beach today. Mother was only eighteen when she and Daddy married, and five years later I was born.

Daddy may have had a rough start, but as God always does, He redeems our past and makes all things new. He promises a good and bright future, one with hope and goodness. I think Daddy wouldn't have been the great man he was if not for his past, because he learned to treat people right—with the dignity and respect they deserved. Instead of becoming bitter about his losses and hardships, by the grace of God he became a blessing to Mother, to me, and to countless others.

STRONG HANDS, SOFT HEART

As you can probably tell, I have always had a tremendous amount of respect and admiration for my daddy. He was a man with strong hands and a soft heart. Daddy worked extremely hard to provide for Mother and me. One day they took me to a store and bought me ten dresses at one time! I was so blessed. Both Mother and Daddy treated me like a queen.

My dad also had a big heart for the community. He volunteered as a deputy sheriff and was a great helper of widows. He would mow lawns for them or repair things around their houses. He also loved to care for servicemen. Mother and

Daddy would often open up our home to those in the military stationed in Baytown. When wives came to visit on the weekends, they would stay in our spare bedroom to help save them from the expenses of hotels. Everyone tried to be patriotic during the war in the 1940s. I loved having people in my house and looked forward to visiting with them.

Daddy would help anyone in need when he could, and that included Mother! Even after a long day at work, he was always willing to help her in the house. He'd usually recruit me to be his assistant, and we would have the best time. Mother might have been a perfectionist when cleaning, but we weren't, and she never knew it!

Out of thirty-seven years working at the oil refinery, Daddy only missed five days of work because of sickness. Hard work goes a long way! You may not be the richest person financially, but like my dad, you can be rich because you know Jesus and build loving relationships. Daddy didn't grow up having a good home life, so he put great effort into being a wonderful husband and father. He honored God and kept a good attitude, even when times were hard. Because he honored God, God honored him.

Daddy worked hard and retired at the age of fifty-seven, mainly so he and Mother could give their time to John and me, our family, and the growing church. My children loved their grandparents and couldn't wait to spend time with them, especially when John and I would travel. Sometimes

I think the children wanted John and me to leave so their grandparents could come to our home. (Those little turkeys!) Because my children were their only grandchildren, they were their grandparents' world, and Mother and Daddy would do anything they could to make things easier for John and me, including cooking and cleaning while we were away. There were nights when we would get home and Daddy would have raked leaves for eight hours at a time!

On top of all they did, Mother and Daddy always gave our children their "old car" when they bought a new one. Paul and Lisa got his gold Buick Skylark with a white roof, and Tamara and Joel got a green Buick LeSabre that was dubbed "the Tank" because it was so big. The children loved it and looked forward to those huge clunkers they would get someday! They were so thankful.

Daddy also volunteered at Lakewood when we were at the old campus. He would drive to Houston and work on plumbing or in the yard all day long. He would do anything that was asked of him.

Even after I had been married for thirty-five years, Daddy used to come to my house nearly every month and bring me money. I used to say, "Daddy, I don't need money. Everything is good with us. John is taking good care of me." But still he would say, "Take it. I want you to have some fun money!" He was incredibly giving. It was one thousand dollars every time and that touched me.

THE POWER OF LOVING AND SERVING

The lesson from my dad that has been etched the deepest in my mind and heart is this: *Our greatest focus should be to love and serve people the way Jesus would.* Daddy didn't get caught up in all of the rules and regulations that are often put on Christians. He simply lived the way the Bible said to live.

He took to heart the words in James 1:27, which tell us that pure and genuine religion in the sight of God is caring for orphans and widows in the midst of their distress. Daddy would care for anyone, no matter who they were or what kind of life they had lived. We should all be careful to not get so caught up in religious rules that we lose sight of why Jesus came in the first place—to love and to serve. The Bible says that real Christianity isn't about perfectly following a set of rules. It's about caring for the hurting people around us, so that through our love they will see Jesus' love, the ultimate love.

> Real Christianity isn't about perfectly following a set of rules. It's about caring for the hurting people around us, so that through our love they will see Jesus' love, the ultimate love.

We are God's best witnesses when we are demonstrating His heart. That's why Jesus lived the way He did! He didn't spend all His time trying to prove that He was God's Son; instead, He let His actions speak for themselves. If we too will let our actions do the talking, we can become the best preachers those around us will ever hear.

RUN YOUR RACE WELL

Both of my parents are in Heaven now. They were married over sixty-eight years when Mother died at the age of eighty-seven. Daddy died a few years later on 9/11 at the age of ninety-six. I'm so glad he didn't have to face the terrible news of that day. These Pilgrims finished their journeys with joy, and I believe Heaven rejoiced to receive them home into their final destination.

Losing my parents was not easy for me, but God helped me. When your loved ones are gone, you miss them, but when you know they fulfilled their purpose and that they are with Jesus, it brings you a great sense of joy to know that they are happy—the happiest they've ever been.

It reminds me of what the apostle Paul said to Timothy in the Bible as he is nearing the end of his life here on earth: "The time for my departure is near. I have fought the good fight, I have finished the race, I have kept the faith. Now there is in store for me the crown of righteousness, which the Lord, the righteous Judge, will award to me on that day" (2 Timothy 4:6–8 NIV).

Paul knew that he had fulfilled God's purposes for his life. He knew that he had run the race God had marked out for him well, and he was ready to receive the reward He had for him. Jesus saw all the good that my parents did for others, and when they met Jesus, I think He said, "Well done, my good and faithful servants."

YOUR STORY IS NOT OVER

Aren't we all pilgrims on a journey? We are headed to our heavenly home, but in the meantime Jesus made this promise: "The thief comes only in order to steal and kill and destroy. I came that they may have *and* enjoy life, and have it in abundance [to the full, till it overflows]" (John 10:10 AMP). Even in the hard times, God says that you can enjoy life and His abundant blessings.

God formed you in your mother's womb and created you for His purposes. As with Daddy, it's not where you start in life that counts. If you will simply give your life to Jesus, He will place you on a new path—a *good* path on which your life can be different and make a difference.

You too may have had a rough start. It hurts to hear the stories of children being abused, neglected, or abandoned and to see men and women devastated by divorce or loss. These things happen and may have happened to you, but your story is not over. Don't allow your past, your hurt, or your tragedy to define your future. You are a pilgrim who is meant to make much progress. You can do it. God is on your side, and He will direct your steps throughout every part of your journey.

As was true for my daddy and mother, along our journeys we too should find ways that we can bless others. It could be something as simple as a smile to a stranger, a helping hand to the elderly, a hospital visit to the sick, or volunteering at your church. There are many ways that you can touch people in your world. All it takes is availability. That's all. Just be available for God to use you.

As I was conducting a prayer service a few years ago, a young woman approached me and whispered in my ear, "I am so ashamed. I was a prostitute, and I gave my heart to the Lord." It touched my heart deeply. I hugged her and prayed for her and asked her to sit on the front row with me. All this young woman needed was someone to care—to be the hands and feet of Jesus. You can be that to someone.

The story of my daddy's childhood always reminds me that God uses ordinary people for extraordinary purposes. My parents were simple people, salt of the earth, solid people, who loved God and people and were loved by everyone in return. God used them greatly in the lives of those around them.

The Bible tells us to never despise the days of "small beginnings, for the LORD rejoices to see the work begin" (Zechariah 4:10 NLT). It doesn't matter how ordinary your upbringing was or is—God can use *you* to do extraordinary things. Small starts can always lead to big finishes if you will allow Him to work through you.

> Small starts can always lead to big finishes if you will allow Him to work through you.

There are plenty of other examples of this besides my own father. In fact, this same small-start/big-finish story line has been present since the beginning of time! We see it all throughout the Bible. Gideon was from a poor family, yet God used him in a great way. It was the same with David. He was just a shepherd boy, one of the lowliest jobs of the day. Esther was from a race that was looked down upon. Her people were threatened to be completely wiped out. *But God* made her the queen over those who plotted against her! Esther was used to bring a mighty deliverance to her people.

One young lady in the church told how she had come to Lakewood two years ago. She had been addicted to drugs, had no self-esteem, and was ashamed of her past. Not only that, she had been in jail five times. But she listened as the Word of God was taught, went to Bible classes during the week, and began to look and think differently. She is now a greeter in the church and beautiful inside and out.

God isn't limited by where you begin. No matter where you come from, with God's help you can become someone who makes a difference in this world. No matter where you are today, He can and will help you finish strong. That's what He did with all of these people, and that's what He did with my daddy. Because he loved Jesus, Daddy's life touched so many people, especially mine. He left behind a wonderful legacy for me.

> God isn't limited by where you begin. No matter where you come from, with God's help you can become someone who makes a difference in this world.

We too can impact other people's lives and leave profound legacies if we choose to live not in the past, but to follow Jesus. One promise you can count on is that God *will* direct your steps on your personal journey.

Life Lesson

You may have had a rough start, but your story is not over. Don't allow your past, your hurt, or your tragedy to define your future. You can do it. God is on your side, and He will direct your steps throughout every part of your journey.

Chapter 2

You Walk Like a Princess

> But you are a chosen people, a royal priest-
> hood, a holy nation, God's special posses-
> sion, that you may declare the praises of
> him who called you out of darkness into his
> wonderful light.
>
> 1 Peter 2:9 NIV

At some point in every girl's life, she dreams of being a princess. She wants to talk like one, dress like one, and walk like
one. Growing up, I was no exception. But while I often imagined myself in a princess ball gown and speaking like royals,
I just couldn't see myself walking like the princesses in the
books I'd read. Instead, I saw myself walking with the slight
limp I'd had since I was young.

Though I've walked with this limp for as long as I can remember, I didn't start out that way. When I was one year old, I was walking on my own as most children do. But before I reached two, I was on my neighbor's porch when I stepped on a rotten board and I fell through and hit a tree stump. My parents said that I cried a little, but I wouldn't walk after that.

Then I began having an elevated temperature, and they realized something unusual was going on in my little body. The doctor first diagnosed me with a virus, but then he realized it was infantile paralysis, or polio as it was later known. My right leg and foot stopped growing normally, and I walked with a limp. I wore a brace on my right leg until I was in the fourth grade. President Franklin Delano Roosevelt was diagnosed with the same virus at the age of thirty-nine and was in a wheelchair the rest of his life.

Mother and Daddy were discouraged by the diagnosis but were determined to make my life the best they possibly could. Every night Daddy would massage my leg to improve the blood circulation. My parents truly did all they could to help their little girl and only child.

I lived life as normally as I could, involving myself in as many activities as possible. I was the color guard in the Lee Brigadiers drum and bugle corps at my high school. I played tennis and other sports that didn't involve too much running. Still, I missed out on activities such as running and shopping for pretty shoes. To this day, I have to buy children's shoes because of my size twelve-and-a-half little foot on the smaller leg. My right foot is a whole inch and a half smaller than the other!

As I got older, the smaller leg grew easier to handle, but I continued to walk with a limp. Though I'd come to accept my little leg and foot and learned to hide it well, it still made me feel somewhat insecure. But one afternoon, many years later, a few words began to change my perspective on the whole situation. They helped me to see what *true royalty* looks like. These words were given to me after I was married to my wonderful husband, John Osteen.

The late Dr. T. L. Osborn, a great man of God, came to visit with John and me, and we were walking together. Out of the clear blue, he stopped, looked at me, and then said to John, "Look at Dodie. She walks like a princess."

As soon as Dr. Osborn said those wonderful words, tears filled the corners of my eyes and began to stream down my cheeks. I had always viewed myself with a focus on my limp, but Dr. Osborn saw me differently. His attitude inspired me to hold my head up high and to see myself through brand-new eyes: *Dodie walks like a princess.*

I decided that I would no longer focus on what I considered my weakness. Just because I have a limp doesn't mean I can't walk like a princess. That day I realized that God was using me despite my shortcomings, and that was a greater testimony than being physically flawless could ever be. I now see that we don't walk like a prince or princess because we're perfect; we walk like one because we're *His*.

Though those life-changing words were spoken over forty years ago, I've *never* forgotten them and I'm certain I never will. Dr. Osborn's encouragement may have been short and simple, but it brought to life something that had weighed on my mind and heart for all of those previous years. It reminded me that God sees me differently than the rest of the world. What some see as a flaw, God sees as beautiful. What some see as a disadvantage, God sees as an advantage, as a divine opportunity to show His power, because His power works best in our weakness (2 Corinthians 12:9).

I have been walking strong all these years, sharing God's love, praying for the sick, traveling all over the world, and doing what Jesus has called me to do. I plan on putting on many more miles because the Bible says God will satisfy us with long life (Psalm 91:16), and I am not satisfied yet!

Dr. Osborn went to Heaven on Valentine's Day 2013. A few days later, I received a letter in the mail from him that made me cry. It was found on his desk and not mailed until after his death. In it, he was encouraging me again. It was written in his own handwriting and will always be so precious to me.

No matter what kind of weakness you have—whether physical, relational, emotional, financial, or any other type—God loves you just the way you are. He sees you as His prince or princess and has a remarkable future planned for you. So don't ever give up!

The Bible says, "For we are His workmanship [His own master work, a work of art], created in Christ Jesus [reborn from above—spiritually transformed, renewed, ready to be used] for good works, which God prepared [for us] beforehand [taking paths which He set], so that we would walk in them [living the good life which He prearranged and made ready for us]" (Ephesians 2:10 AMP).

You were designed by God to be just the way you are (Psalm 139:13–18). He made you the way He did for a reason. If your Creator is the Creator of the universe, why would you criticize His handiwork? Instead of finding fault with yourself, I encourage you to hold your head up high and be exactly who God created you to be. Don't allow a negative self-image to dwell in you. Instead, let God shine through you (Isaiah 60:1)!

GENTLE HANDS, SWEET WORDS

It's amazing how words as simple as those I received from Dr. Osborn can heal our hearts. I have never believed there is any truth in the phrase "Sticks and stones may break my bones, but words will never hurt me." Words really have the power to make or break us, inflicting deep hurt and harm or blessing and encouragement.

For seventeen years, my oldest son, Paul, worked as a

surgeon in Little Rock, Arkansas, and still performs surgery on the mission field today. For several months out of the year, he serves the people in very remote and tiny hospitals all over Africa. One day, after having worked at the Tenwek Hospital in Kenya, East Africa, for an extended period, Paul noticed that people were traveling all the way to Tenwek even though they had a hospital closer to their villages. Finally he asked one of the women why she traveled so far for treatment.

"Because at Tenwek Hospital the staff's hands are gentle and their words are sweet," she answered.

How wonderful! People are attracted to those who make their words sweet.

Are you building others up or tearing them down with your words? How are you talking about your life and situations? Sometimes we are our own worst critics. If you will speak life-giving words of faith found in God's Word, you will be amazed at where it will lead you and those you love.

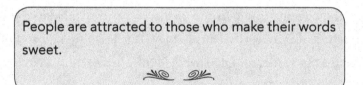

People are attracted to those who make their words sweet.

Jesus is the perfect example of a life giver. While on this earth, He was always kind and His words were always gracious. When we imitate Him, we lift people up. A smile, a kind word, or a simple act of love is always sure to lift someone's spirit. Of course, with some you have to choose to look beyond the natural to encourage them. Maybe what you see isn't worth praising at that moment. If so, then focus on what you want to see in the future!

For many years, Jesse Gallardo, a faithful family friend, served John as a volunteer assistant. Jesse is such a blessing to our family. He had a negative upbringing and went through a painful divorce, but he became an amazing single dad who raised four children. God restored his life and gave him a beautiful wife, Martha, who also had a child of her own. Jesse was always so proud of his children. His son, Jeff, was a great football player in high school. In case you're not aware, football is big in Texas, but it was even bigger to this dad than to most!

One day Jesse asked John to attend one of Jeff's games. The opposing team kicked the football to Jeff, but the defenders were on him so tightly that he had nowhere to run and was tackled quickly. Jeff took one step to the left, one to the right, and then went down in the arms of several tacklers. John thought it was a pretty routine play. But Jesse turned to him, smiled a big smile, and declared, "Did you see those two good moves?"

That story is just a glimpse into how Jesse saw his children. He always focused on the good—on who they could be and what they could do over who they were and what they were doing at that moment. He called things that were not yet as though they were! God did the same thing for Abraham when he and Sarah were unable to have children. He changed his name from Abram to Abraham, which means "father of many nations" (Genesis 17:5). God called Abraham and Sarah the way He saw them and intended them to be. And as you probably know, Abraham and Sarah fulfilled what God had spoken. They went on to have their promised child, Isaac.

Our words are powerful and have creative force. Scripture says that our tongues can bring forth death or life and that we are to encourage one another daily (Proverbs 18:21; Hebrews 3:13), just as Jesse did with his son, just as God did with Abraham and Sarah, and just as Dr. Osborn did with me.

One word can put people on their feet! That day with Dr. Osborn, my confidence increased tremendously. Today I walk like a princess. I started seeing myself not as I thought I appeared when I looked in the mirror, but as how the King of kings sees me, His daughter, His princess. I pray you do the same!

One word can put people on their feet!

KEEP THE RIGHT FOCUS

When I was young, and even after I was first married, I used to avoid watching myself walk in a storefront or mirror or anything reflective. If I passed one, I would just look the other way. I often wondered why my husband would be interested in me, a young lady with the flaw I had. But John didn't even see it. He would always tell me how beautiful I was and how much he loved me.

My children also say they never noticed my leg being small when they were growing up. And my grandchildren tell me that they didn't even realize that I limped until their parents pointed it out to them! In fact, one day my grand-daughter Christiana saw me on the platform and whispered to her mother, April, "Look at Grandmother's little leg. It's so cute!"

That blessed me so much. It made me realize that often-times others don't even see the weaknesses we are so concerned or even obsessed about. The more we focus on our flaws and talk about them, the bigger they become to us and to everyone around us. Just the other day I was walking and saw my shadow. I noticed that I limped a little, and I imme-diately thought, *Look at Dodie, she walks like a princess.* Dr. Osborn's five simple but life-changing words spoken over me forty years earlier had risen up in my spirit. That was a special moment to me.

It's also a true picture of how we should see one another. We're called to focus on others' strengths, not their weak-nesses. We're called to view any imperfections as an oppor-tunity for something great to be born. So I encourage you to focus your attention on your strengths and on the strengths of those you love. When we have our focus right, God can use us in powerful ways.

IN EVERYTHING, GIVE THANKS!

At Lakewood, I conduct most of the funeral services, which is something I love to do. Not long ago at a funeral home visitation, I met a doctor who was in a wheelchair. I asked someone about his condition, and they said he had had polio in the 1950s. He had contracted a different type of polio than the type I had and had been in an iron lung. After he recovered, he went to medical school. I admire him because he didn't let a physical handicap keep him from doing what God had put in his heart.

I don't meet many others who contracted polio, so I really wanted to speak with him. I introduced myself to him and to his wife and told him my story. Then I showed him my little leg. His response was one I will never forget. He looked at me from his seated position in the wheelchair and said these simple words: "Yes, but it works." I felt so ashamed for the times I had complained about having a small leg and foot and about not wearing pretty shoes. He was in a wheelchair, and I was the complainer!

Next time you find yourself having a pity party over what you don't have, remind yourself of what you do have. There is *always* something for which to be thankful. This doctor could have focused on his limitations, on the fact that he was bound to a wheelchair. But I love his attitude and confidence, because he chose to see his potential instead. Being in a wheelchair didn't nullify the fact that he was intelligent and had a desire to be a physician. He didn't allow his weaknesses to keep him from making this world a better place.

> Next time you find yourself having a pity party over what you don't have, remind yourself of what you do have.

NOTHING IS TOO SMALL

In John 6, we're told the story of a huge crowd of people who had spent the entire day listening to Jesus. Toward the end of the day, they began to grow hungry. Jesus was mindful of that fact, just as He is of any needs we have today. So He said to the disciples, "You give them something to eat." Their response was that unless they were to go and buy food for the multitude, all they had were five loaves of bread and two fish from one little boy (John 6:8)!

But that didn't faze Jesus! All He needed was a willing heart. He blessed the boy's small lunch and handed it to the disciples to give out to the people. Miraculously, it continued to multiply until over five thousand men were fed, plus all of the women and children! What a sight that must have been! No one left hungry that day. Plus there were twelve baskets of fragments left over!

I'm sure the disciples were skeptical as they focused on the boy's tiny amount of food compared to the magnitude of the hungry mouths. How could those few loaves and fish possibly provide nourishment for all those people? I've been a mother to teenage boys who liked to eat. I know I would have been a little doubtful! That's the same way some of us see our lives— as insignificant, as not having what it takes to make much of a difference. But nothing could be further from the truth!

If you will offer what you have to Jesus with a willing heart, He will multiply it. He doesn't care if you've been labeled a complete failure by the world; He can make your life one of great value. All that's required is that you offer it to Him. God doesn't care what you've done or where you've been! He just wants you.

Let me ask you a question. How do you walk? Are you limping through life because of your past or because you are focusing on what you are not or what you do not have? Is your head hung down in defeat and discouragement? It's time to lift it up high and to begin to believe what your heavenly Father says about you. You are wonderfully and fearfully created for His good pleasure (Psalm 139:14). You are chosen by God as His special treasure. Don't allow what you consider your weaknesses to keep you from living life to its fullest. Today is your day to walk like a prince or princess!

Life Lesson

God sees you differently than how the rest of the world sees you. What some see as a flaw, God sees as beautiful. What some see as a disadvantage, God sees as an advantage, as a divine opportunity to show His power. He loves you just the way you are and sees you as His prince or princess. We don't walk like a prince or princess because we're perfect; we walk like one because we are *His*.

Chapter 3

A Legacy of Faith

As for me and my family, we will serve the
LORD.

Joshua 24:15 NLT

When I was five years old, my mother and daddy visited Central Baptist Church, which was only a few blocks from our house. They gave their lives to Jesus, which set the stage for me to receive Him as my Lord and Savior as well. It was in that church that a foundation of faith was built in my heart. I'm thankful for parents who took me to church.

I went to Sunday school and church every week and learned so much about my heavenly Father. One day when I was thirteen years old, I read an article by someone who predicted that the world was going to come to an end. I went into the garage where Daddy was changing the oil in our car and expressed my concern about the article I had read and about my future. The very next Sunday I couldn't wait for the altar call. I knew that I wanted to accept Jesus into my heart. I did, and it was the best decision I have ever made.

That day is when Jesus changed my life from the inside out. When I prayed the salvation prayer, I became a new creation in Christ Jesus. He forgave my past sins and delivered me out of the kingdom of darkness into the kingdom of His marvelous light. I became a child of God and the Holy Spirit made His home within me. I have peace with God, and I know I will spend eternity in Heaven. It's wonderful to know God on a personal basis!

Since the age of thirteen, I have walked with the Lord, which is a long time, and it just keeps getting better and better! He is my Savior, deliverer, healer, and friend. I don't know how I would live life without Him. You too can know Jesus, no matter what your age or past. God longs to be close to you. (See Appendix 1.)

If you are a parent, I hope you realize how important it is for you to take your children to a good Bible-believing church when they are young. Even if you don't think they understand or care to understand, know that one day it will pay off and they will be so thankful. The seeds you are planting will eventually sprout. So be sure to plant good things! It's much easier to mold children when they are young rather than when they become teenagers. Still, no matter how old they are, it's never too late for you or them!

SHINE THE LIGHT

In Acts 16 is the wonderful story of the apostle Paul and Silas who had been unjustly cast into the inner dungeon of a prison for declaring the truth of the Gospel. They were put in stocks, singing and worshiping the Lord at midnight when a great earthquake suddenly shook the prison, opening the doors and loosing the prisoners' chains. Then the keeper of the prison, supposing the prisoners had fled, drew his sword and was about to kill himself. Paul called out with a loud voice, saying, "Do yourself no harm, for we are all here." When the prison keeper brought them out, he said, "Sirs, what must I do to be saved?" So they said, "Believe on the Lord Jesus Christ, and you will be saved, you and your household." Then they spoke the word of the Lord to him and to all who were in his house, and they all came to Jesus.

With their backs bleeding and feet in stocks, Paul and Silas had been praying and singing praises to God! Anybody can sing in the sunshine, but people of faith can sing no matter what is happening. It may be dark around you, but it is light on the inside. When we praise Him in the darkness, He'll bring us out into the sunshine!

Do you see that the testimony of Paul and Silas was so clear that the jailer desperately wanted the life of Jesus for himself and his household? The jailer was saying, "I want to be like you. I want to have the joy you have. I want to have the victory you have. I want to have that something you have. How do I get it?"

Paul's answer was simple and clear: "Believe on the Lord Jesus Christ." Not believe just *in* Jesus, but *on* Him. Trust yourself to Him. Commit your whole life to Him as your Lord and Savior, and you shall be saved. And then here's what thrills me as well, "And your household!" It's not just good for Daddy; it's good for the whole house! God wants our households saved!

Do not discount the power of your faith and influence. It's amazing what one believer can do in a household. See how the jailer who got saved asked Paul to come and preach to his household, and everyone in his household got baptized. It's wonderful what one saved person who lets his or her light shine can do for Jesus!

When John first put his faith in Jesus, his brothers and sisters spent a lot of time in nightclubs, making decisions that went against the Bible, and had no interest in the things of God. As a new believer, he was concerned that his family would criticize him, and he wasn't sure what to say to them. But instead of going out with them, John would stay home and get out the big old family Bible and read it. He said he didn't understand much of what he read at the time, but he was trying to let his light shine as best he could.

One of John's sisters, Mary, was the first to realize that something was different in his life. One night she was going out to a nightclub and came and stood right beside him. Then she said, "John, why do you stay home and read the Bible now and don't go out with us?" He didn't look up, but he said, "Mary, I've given my heart to Jesus, and I'm not going to the world anymore!" He thought she would make fun of him, but nothing came out of her mouth. So he looked up, and tears were running down her face. She said, "John, do you think Jesus would save somebody like me?" He said, "Oh, Mary, He will. He will." In that moment Mary knelt at the dining room table and passed out of darkness into light, out of death into eternal life.

John's first convert was his own sister. How precious!

And one by one the other members of John's family came to Jesus. Next came John's two brothers, Jack and Odell, who gave their hearts to the Lord. Odell became a Methodist pastor. His mother got saved, and his other two sisters, Hazel and Jacque, also were saved later. Jacque came running into the house one night and said, "I was in a tent revival, and I gave my heart to Jesus!"

John's father wasn't so easy. He said, "When you're dead, you're dead like a dog. Roll me over in a ditch. That's all there is to life." John said, "Daddy, if that were true, I'll never bother you again. But you've got to live on forever somewhere." Thank God, he got saved as well and became a faithful member and usher in his local church.

THE POWER OF YOUR EXAMPLE

Similar to the prison keeper's family and John's family, after our little Pilgrim family came to know Jesus, we were set on a new path forever. Sundays with my parents are some of the most cherished memories I have. Mother went to church often, but she was sick and couldn't attend every week. Daddy and I did, though, and I treasured the times we had together.

Because my parents grew up in the Depression, they were very frugal with their money, but that didn't keep them from faithfully giving their 10 percent tithe to the Lord every week. In fact, Daddy kept a log of how much he gave to his church. After he went to Heaven, we found his tiny brown spiral notebook that listed every penny he gave to the Lord. What a legacy that is for my children, my grandchildren, and me.

When my granddaughter Andrea was little, I gave her the bedroom suite my parents had bought me when I was five years old. Years later, when she and her mother, Tamara, were packing up her belongings for college, they found a canceled tithe check he must have lost at the very bottom of the dresser. It was addressed to Central Baptist Church, dated August 13, 1956, and was for twelve dollars! I was so touched. No matter how large or small the tithe amount was that week, Daddy *never* missed a Sunday of giving!

When I was in junior high school, oil was discovered on the property on which our home was built. They put an oil derrick on the lot, and Mother and Daddy were paid five hundred dollars a month for a long time. Back in the 1940s, that was a lot of money! I really believe Daddy's commitment to honor

God with his giving was the reason that we were always so well taken care of.

Mother, Daddy, and I lived in an older house until I was five years old. One summer day they took me to stay with my grandmother. I didn't know it, but while I was gone, they were decorating a new house that they had built. It was a lovely three-bedroom house, which to us was a palace, even though it was probably only twelve hundred square feet. At that time, the lot and the house cost only twenty-five hundred dollars. Isn't that amazing? Mother and Daddy lived in that little house until they went to Heaven. We have a lot of great memories with our children going to their grandparents' home for visits and Mother's delicious Thanksgiving dinners.

My parents set an excellent example for me in the areas of faith and finances. The Bible says, "A generous person will prosper; whoever refreshes others will be refreshed" (Proverbs 11:25 NIV). You don't have to be wealthy to be generous. We sure weren't! But as you bless others, God will bless you. As I grew up and began earning money, I always tithed too because I saw firsthand that when I put God first in my life, He always took care of me.

It is the same for all of us. The Bible says to "seek the Kingdom of God above all else, and live righteously, and he will give you everything you need" (Matthew 6:33 NLT). It says that those who honor God, He will honor (1 Samuel 2:30). If you are struggling financially or in any other area, I encourage you to begin putting God first in everything. Put God first in your finances, in your relationships, and in the use of your time, and you will be amazed at how your situations will turn around! God always keeps His promises.

> Put God first in your finances, in your relationships, and in the use of your time, and you will be amazed at how your situations will turn around!

I once heard someone say that children are little video cameras on legs, watching every move we make. Some days as a mom that definitely felt true for me! It's so important to set a godly example for our children and grandchildren. We should always make it one that gives God our best and trusts Him to fulfill His promises. If you are a young parent, take a stand now so that your children will have examples to look back on. If you are older, know that it is never too late to start.

I encourage you to find a good church that teaches the Bible and take your family every Sunday. Let them see you read God's Word and pray, and read it with them regularly. Let them watch you depend on Him in tough times. Joshua, who led the nation of Israel into the Promised Land, said, "As for me and my family, we will serve the LORD" (Joshua 24:15 NLT). Though none of us can do everything right, every one of us can do our best every day. By doing these things, your life will speak so loudly!

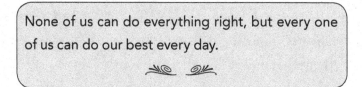

None of us can do everything right, but every one of us can do our best every day.

Even if you didn't have a Christ-centered life modeled for you as a child, don't let your children grow up to say the same thing. Set a new legacy for your family. *Today* can be the day that changes your children's future, and you can be the one to change it!

Our little family was a happy family, and I credit that to serving the Lord. We had our share of challenges, but we were not alone in facing them. When you know Jesus, you always have hope. And He is ever present to give His infinite wisdom, for in Him "are hidden all the treasures of wisdom and knowledge" (Colossians 2:3).

When you know Jesus, you always have hope.

James reminds us, "If any of you lacks wisdom, you should ask God, who gives generously to all without finding fault, and it will be given to you" (James 1:5 NIV). Have you taken time to ask God for wisdom for your family, job, or the decisions you have before you? God is available to you, anytime and anywhere.

The Bible states that our bodies are temples of the Holy Spirit. He lives and dwells in us because God sent Him to be our "Helper (Comforter, Advocate, Intercessor—Counselor, Strengthener, Standby)" (John 14:16 AMP). Do you see how equipped God has made you? So don't just go through the motions of life—realize who you are in Christ and what you have in Him. The greater one lives in you! No matter what you may be going through today, you can make it because God's grace is sufficient for you today, tomorrow, and the next day!

Life Lesson

Do not discount the power of your faith and influence. It's amazing what one believer can do in a household. Even if you didn't grow up in a godly home, don't let your children grow up to say the same thing. Set a new legacy for your family and the generation to come. *Today* can be the day that changes your children's future, and you can be the one to change it!

Chapter 4

Touch of the Master's Hand

⁂

If you confess with your mouth the Lord
Jesus and believe in your heart that God
has raised Him from the dead, you will be
saved.

Romans 10:9

It was during high school that John met a young man named
Sam Martin, who became his best friend. As Sam would say,
they were "two lost sinners living in sin." That is, until Sam
got saved. Once Sam dedicated his life to God, he began to
change the way he lived. He also began witnessing to their
classmates, which seemed to embarrass John. Sam would
write scriptures on the blackboard between classes and talk
to people about Jesus in the hallways.

After Sam's transformation, John avoided him as much as

possible. He said that Sam constantly told him about the love of God, but he wouldn't listen to him. Anytime Sam would invite him to church, he would be conveniently busy. But Sam had his heart set on John and kept after him to give his life to Jesus. Though Sam's words might have been brushed off at the beginning, they stuck with John when he needed them most.

John used to tell me the story of his "coming home from a nightclub at two o'clock in the morning, in South Fort Worth, Texas, lost and undone, without God or His Son. I began to think about time . . . eternity . . . Heaven. *Where would I spend eternity?*" When he got home, he took a quilt from the house and laid it outside on the lawn. He lay down and gazed up at the stars and the moon and the universe. It was then he was convinced that there was a God, and God began to deal with him about letting Him into his life.

After a few minutes of gazing into the heavens, he went back inside and grabbed the big family Bible that was sitting on the coffee table. When he opened it up, it fell open to a famous painting of Jesus standing and knocking on a door. Under the picture were the words: "Behold, I stand at the door and knock. If anyone hears My voice and opens the door, I will come in to him and dine with him, and he with Me" (Revelation 3:20). In that moment John understood that Jesus was knocking and had been knocking on the door of his life for some time.

Still, John didn't know what to do about it, but he did remember Sam—the high school friend who had talked to him about Jesus many times before. So as soon as the sun came up, he called Sam and told him that he wanted to go to church with him that Sunday morning.

Sam always said that the following Sunday morning, John beat *him* to church. But when the altar call was given, John said he felt as though his feet had been nailed to the floor and he couldn't move. When Sam realized he wasn't going to go forward, he grabbed John's arm and walked with him. There Sam was again, standing by John's side when he lacked the courage to stand on his own. What a great friend!

When they reached the altar, the pastor of the church asked John if he wanted to confess Jesus as his Lord and Savior in front of the congregation. John hung his head and replied, "But, Pastor, I've lived a bad life."

The pastor immediately responded, "That's not what I asked you. I asked: 'Do you want to confess Jesus Christ as your Savior?'"

In that moment Sam said an obvious change occurred in John. His entire countenance suddenly was transformed. I believe it's because that was the moment in which he finally understood the grace of God. He lifted his head, pulled his shoulders back, looked straight into the pastor's eyes, and said with confidence, "Absolutely." With that word, John took his first step to becoming a man of faith.

Thank God for Sam Martin, because he never gave up on John, just as God never gives up on us. Even when John gave Sam every reason to walk away and let him figure things out on his own, he didn't. He stayed faithful to believe in John and in the purpose God had for him.

We all have people in our lives that we see have great potential, but who are not yet serving Jesus. Maybe it's a relative, a coworker, or a friend. It's easy to assume that they have everything all figured out and are happy enough. They may even ignore your advice or make fun of how God has worked in your life, but don't give up on them. Let the story of John and Sam encourage you that hearts can be changed by one touch of the Master's hand.

As my beloved husband's friend did, keep believing that the person you are reaching out to will be like the prodigal son, who comes to his senses and remembers how you ministered to them. They will remember the words you spoke and the love that you showed them. And they will be forever grateful that you stood by them and believed in them, even when they didn't believe for themselves. It just takes one person to make a difference. You can be that one! People read your life as they would read a Bible.

People read your life as they would read a Bible.

THE TOUCH OF THE MASTER'S HAND

There was a poem that John often quoted from memory and loved to share with people because he felt it spoke of what

God had so graciously done in his life. This poem about an old violin, "The Touch of the Master's Hand," was written in 1921 by Myra Brooks Welch, who was called "the Poet with the Singing Soul." She said that she felt this poem was a gift from God to her, so she sent it anonymously to her church news bulletin. Many years later, after the poem's popularity had spread far and wide, it was discovered that she was its author. As you read it, I think you'll understand why it touched John's heart so deeply:

'Twas battered and scarred, and the auctioneer
Thought it hardly worth his while
To waste his time on the old violin,
But he held it up with a smile.
"What am I bidden, good people," he cried,
"Who'll start the bidding for me?"
"A dollar, a dollar. Then two! Only two?
Two dollars, and who'll make it three?"

"Three dollars, once; three dollars twice,
Going for three . . ." But no,
From the room, far back, a gray-haired man
Came forward and picked up the bow;
Then wiping the dust from the old violin,
And tightening the loosened strings,
He played a melody pure and sweet
As a caroling angel sings.

The music ceased, and the auctioneer
With a voice that was quiet and low,
Said: "What am I bid for the old violin?"
And he held it up with the bow.
"A thousand dollars, and who'll make it two?
Two thousand! And who'll make it three?
Three thousand, once; three thousand, twice,
And going and gone," said he.

The audience cheered, but some of them cried,
"We do not quite understand.
What changed its worth?" Swift came the reply.
"The touch of the Master's hand."
And many a man with life out of tune,
And battered and scarred with sin,
Is auctioned cheap to a thoughtless crowd
Much like the old violin.

A "mess of pottage," a glass of wine,
A game—and he travels on.
He is "going" once, and "going" twice,
He is "going" and almost "gone."
But the Master comes, and the foolish crowd
Never can quite understand
The worth of a soul and the change that is wrought
By the touch of the Master's hand.

AMAZING GRACE

Grace is such a beautiful gift; it's the greatest gift we can ever receive. And the best part is, it's free to us! The Bible says that we get this gift not because of anything we have ever done or will ever do, but because of what Jesus did on the cross for us so many years ago (Ephesians 2:8–9). We don't deserve it, we can't deserve it, and we don't have to deserve it! It is unearned and unmerited. There are no strings attached. We simply have to accept and receive it.

> Grace is such a beautiful gift; it's the greatest gift we can ever receive.

Once we fully understand and accept this grace that Jesus offers, then our entire life will change, as did John's life. We'll have a new hope in our hearts that the Lord will take care of our future. Through grace we find that God has an amazing purpose for tomorrow regardless of what happened yesterday.

God loves you *no matter what*. Once you have repented of your sins, He deletes the past sins and wipes your slate clean through the blood Jesus shed on the cross. You can forget your past sins and live for the future, ignoring the thoughts that you aren't good enough to be a child of God. You can lift your head up, put your shoulders back, and get ready to walk into the incredible future God has prepared for you!

A CHANGED LIFE CHANGES LIVES

Once my husband had a firm grasp on the concept of God's grace, he realized that part of it was the grace to help him change his lifestyle. The Holy Spirit began to convict him of some things he needed to change. He wanted to please Jesus, even in what some would consider small things!

For example, when he worked at the theater, he would often eat the candy and popcorn he was supposed to be selling. Years after he accepted Jesus, he remembered and felt convicted for what he had done. He drove to Fort Worth to pay the owner for what he had eaten without paying. The owner would not accept any money, but appreciated his sincerity! He also owed money for a suit he bought, and he paid that off too.

Soon after he gave his heart to Jesus, John began to preach at the age of seventeen! He felt God's call to the ministry on his life. From that point on, he spoke wherever he could. His first pulpit was on the streets! From nursing homes, Bible studies, and street corners, John would preach wherever people would listen. He would ride a bus, walk, or do anything just to preach the good news about Jesus.

One day a lady in a nursing home gave him a quarter for her gratitude. It was the first offering he ever received. Her name was Mrs. Smedley and he never forgot it. He didn't get a paycheck for preaching, but he didn't mind one bit! God's love was burning so strongly in his heart that he just wanted to share it with everyone.

John's lifestyle change spoke as loudly to those around him as did his words. The first people who began to take notice of the change were his family, particularly his older sister Mary. In the previous chapter, I described how she came to faith through John's testimony, which was followed by the rest of his family.

I love that story because it shows that when we change, people notice it. We may assume that people are going to ridicule us when we talk about Jesus, and maybe some will. But many times people are more open than we think they will be. Sometimes they just need us to love them and tell the truth about what Jesus can do for them. Jesus healed me of cancer, and I tell people everywhere about it. If they don't like it, they don't have to come around me! I don't mean you should be rude or obnoxious, but please, never be ashamed!

When John was first saved, he tried to tell his father about Jesus, but his father never wanted to listen. But one day, years later, while John was preaching in Dallas, he saw his prayer answered. In the middle of his message, his father came walking down the aisle and up on the platform. He interrupted John's message and said, "I need to finish now what I started years ago."

That day John discovered that years before his dad had been

caught in a snowstorm. As he thought he was literally freezing to death, he looked up at the sky and said, "God, if You're real, get me out of this and I'll serve You." But after he was safe back at home, he reneged on the promise he had made. Thank God for His grace and mercy and patience!

It's never good to put off accepting Jesus. It's the most important decision we will ever make in our lives, because it determines where we will spend eternity. Heaven will be wonderful and being with Jesus throughout eternity will be glorious beyond our wildest dreams.

After he was saved, John's daddy's life changed tremendously. He became an usher in his church, and when he died, they found tracts on salvation in his suit pockets. Think about it: A stubborn man who never believed in Jesus became so determined to convince others of God's love that he would hand out Gospel messages. That's the difference Jesus can make!

PREPARED BY GOD

As John further sought God about his future, he felt that part of His plan was to complete what he had left unfinished—his high school education. Before he got saved, he made Cs and Ds in school, but after he made As and Bs. Then he continued on to pursue his college degree. It's hard to describe how big this step was for my husband, because he certainly did not have enough money to put himself through college. But he trusted God to provide, and He did!

John hitchhiked to John Brown University in Siloam Springs, Arkansas. He worked hard and became an excellent student. He left there and went to Northern Baptist Theological Seminary in Chicago and received his master's degree. While he was there, he worked hard shoveling snow to pay for his tuition.

If God calls you to do something, He will always provide you with what you need to do it. The apostle Paul states, "God will supply every need of yours according to his riches in glory in Christ Jesus" (Philippians 4:19 ESV). Whether it is finances, resources, relationships, or whatever it may be, trust God with it. He will always equip you to do what He asks of you.

> If God calls you to do something, He will always provide you with what you need to do it.
>
> ━◦◦━

Everywhere John preached, people loved him. He delivered passionate evangelistic messages, and people always gave their hearts to Jesus. I loved listening to my husband's messages too. I marveled at how he was so fiery and yet still so kind and loving to people. Out of all the forty-four years, four months, and six days of our marriage, I can honestly say that I never heard him preach a bad sermon, yet he still was so humble. Even up until his last Sunday message, his first question when we got in the car was, "How did I do?"

When John moved and became the pastor of my home church in Baytown, people often referred to him as "the Billy Graham of Baytown." But I just knew him as John, my sweetheart, who was not just the greatest preacher, but also the greatest man I had ever known.

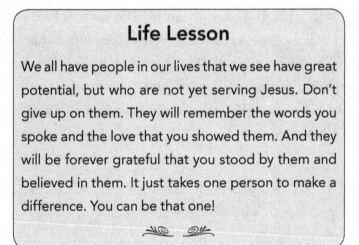

Life Lesson

We all have people in our lives that we see have great potential, but who are not yet serving Jesus. Don't give up on them. They will remember the words you spoke and the love that you showed them. And they will be forever grateful that you stood by them and believed in them. It just takes one person to make a difference. You can be that one!

Chapter 5

Marrying My Pastor

Take delight in the LORD, and he will give
you your heart's desires.

Psalm 37:4 NLT

As I grew up, I had a lot of fun and lots of friends, and since I
had no siblings, I was allowed to have my friends over to our
house often. I also used to love visiting my grandparents. My
grandmother's name was Ida and she had a twin sister named
Ada. Every time I'd go see her, as soon as I walked through the
door, she would get out a potato and start peeling it because she
knew that I loved fried potatoes. I was her only grandchild for
six years, so I might have been a little spoiled!

I was very involved in school. I took accordion lessons and
actually played at school, in special programs, and even on
the radio one time. But today I don't even remember where

middle C is! I went to Robert E. Lee High School and joined the Lee Brigadiers drum and bugle corps and was a color guard. Even though I had lots of friends, I had no boyfriends. I was shy when it came to boys.

One of my favorite things to do today is get together with my high school classmates several times a year for lunch at a restaurant in Baytown. There are about forty of us still living, and we have a good time visiting and catching up on one another's lives. They are precious to me.

When I was a little girl, I used to say that someday I was going to marry a preacher, have four or five children, and become a nurse. Sure enough, after high school I attended the Lillie Jolly School of Nursing affiliated with Memorial Hospital in Houston. I absolutely loved it. It was in downtown Houston, right by the library and city hall. I lived there for three years. It was in that school I realized that taking care of sick people was one of my greatest passions.

GOD WILL BRING YOU THE RIGHT MATE

While in nursing school, I would go home about once a month, and I always attended our church on the weekends. There were several pastors at Central Baptist Church throughout the years, but at this time the pastor was John Osteen. I had listened to him many times and truly believed he was one of the best preachers I had ever heard.

It didn't take long for the church to begin growing once Pastor Osteen took over, and it seemed to be thriving under his leadership. But on one weekend visit, I heard that our pastor was going through an unwanted and hurtful divorce. I was so busy in school that I didn't hear much about it, but I remember feeling compassion for him. I hoped he wouldn't have to leave our church or the denomination because he was such a great preacher.

Well, time went by and I'd often see Pastor Osteen visiting people in the hospital I worked at in Houston. We would speak casually, but I thought nothing of it. Then one weekend when I was home, I spoke with him in front of the church. Later he told me that after that conversation, Jesus spoke to his heart that someday I would be his wife. John told me that at the time he said to himself, "That little thing doesn't know it yet, but I am going to marry her." By this time I loved nursing so much that I had decided I wanted to be a career nurse and never get married. Boy, did that ever change! God definitely had other plans, and they were much better for me!

As the weeks passed, I noticed that Pastor Osteen was at the hospital *a lot*. I thought, *That pastor must have the sickest people in his church!* It took me a while to realize that he was coming to see me! Not long after this realization, we began dating. He was the first man I truly dated and the only man I ever loved.

It's so important to trust that God will bring you the right mate. He has someone specific in mind for you, and He will cause your paths to cross at just the right time. Trying to force relationships only leads to unnecessary pain, so be confident in God's timing. He alone knows who you need to walk alongside you and who can help you fulfill His purposes for your life.

> God alone knows who you need to walk alongside you and who can help you fulfill His purposes for your life.
>
> ❧ ☙

John and I dated several months, and throughout that time I continued to call him "Brother Osteen." Finally one night he said, "Will you please quit calling me Brother Osteen and just call me John?" I did, though I must admit I felt a little uncomfortable! But it didn't take long for "John" to develop into "Sweetheart" and "Darling," and that was a lot more fun!

I was still in nursing school while we were dating, but John would come to Houston to see me or I would go home and see him. He came over to my parents' house a lot, and we'd just sit on the porch and visit. My mother and daddy loved him. One of my favorite memories was when John came to the hospital on Valentine's Day and brought me a beautiful necklace and earrings. They were not expensive, but it thrilled me. I still have the earrings!

We set our wedding date after praying and knowing that it was God's will for us to marry. I wasn't sure what the future had in store for us, but my love for him was so strong. I really felt God would be pleased with our marriage. I knew that John needed to be restored, and I felt as though God was calling me to be a part of that as his wife.

I knew nothing about being a pastor's wife, and I felt that I was being ushered into an entirely new realm, but I knew I loved John. One day before our wedding I was a little discouraged by the thought of pastoring, so I told him, "Sweetheart, I can't play the piano. I can't sing. I can't teach a class. I can't do anything a pastor's wife is supposed to do."

John replied, "Dodie, I'm not marrying you to do all that. I'm marrying you because I love you and I want you to love me. I like you just the way you are." That was easy to do. He was so lovable. And it set me free and made me know that I could just be myself. I did not have to be like any other pastor's wife.

My graduation from nursing school was in August and my state board exam was September 9 and 10. By the grace of God I passed the first time and married my pastor the next week on September 17, 1954.

FAIRY TALES DO COME TRUE

John and I had a fairy-tale wedding at Central Baptist Church. I felt as though I was a queen with my king. John asked Dr. Kyle Yates, the pastor at Second Baptist Church in Houston, to perform our wedding. John was unsure about asking because of the divorce, but Dr. Yates was more than willing to do it. He was such a wonderful man!

We went to Estes Park, Colorado, on our honeymoon, and it was wonderful. Mother and Daddy gave us twenty-five hundred dollars for the trip. I told John I wanted us to come back with half of it, and we did. He still had to pay off loans from the seminary as well as a few other things, and he really didn't have a big salary. But we did have a beautiful parsonage, so we used the money to buy all new furniture. We also had a beautiful baby-blue-and-white Chevrolet that Mother and Daddy had given me for graduation from nursing school. It was so special to me.

When John and I married, I was twenty-one and he was thirty-three. He had a sweet little eight-year-old son, Justin, whom he adored and always paid child support to every month. Justin went on to serve our country in the military as a translator. He is a brilliant man and has worked with churches for years.

The people in our church were wonderful to us. A few church members left because of John's divorce, but we understood that it's a hard issue and we forgave those who made unkind comments. We need to be careful and compassionate in what we say about and to divorced people. Those who have been divorced and gone through all kinds of heartache have had enough hurt without anyone's additional comments.

I surely don't encourage divorce, but please never write

off people who go through one. Sometimes they can't do a thing in the world about it, and God is a God of grace, mercy, and restoration. God forgives divorce and heals those who are bruised and battered by divorce. Jesus commanded us to love them and help them, not to condemn them. Jesus said, "For God did not send His Son into the world to condemn the world, but that the world through Him might be saved" (John 3:17). He also said that in this world we would have many tribulations (John 16:33), and that includes divorce. But no matter what we go through, God can restore us. He certainly restored my husband!

> No matter what we go through, God can restore us. He is a God of grace, mercy, and forgiveness.

After we were married five months, we found out we were going to have our first child. We were so excited! By November of the following year, we had a beautiful little boy, Paul Kent. Within the next ten years, we had four more children: Lisa Kelley, Tamara Ann, Joel Scott, and April Leigh. These five children became our biggest blessing!

Once I married John and became a pastor's wife, eventually my life passion translated into praying for the sick. I see now that during nursing school, God was preparing me for what I would do for the rest of my life in the church. He was moving in my heart from the time I was five years old as I dreamed of caring for those who were hurting. God always plants desires in our hearts for a reason, and He will be faithful to bring them to pass. It might not happen as we expect, but if not, we can be sure that His way is greater!

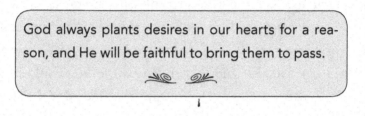

God always plants desires in our hearts for a reason, and He will be faithful to bring them to pass.

Life Lesson

It's so important to trust that God will bring you the right mate. He has someone specific in mind for you, and He will cause your paths to cross at just the right time. Trying to force relationships only leads to unnecessary pain, so be confident in God's timing. It might not happen as we expect, but if not, we can be sure that His way is greater!

Chapter 6

Keep the Laughter in Your Marriage

Above all, clothe yourselves with love, which
binds us all together in perfect harmony.

Colossians 3:14 NLT

I was blessed with an amazing husband and marriage, but just like everyone else, John and I had our times of disagreement. During those times, I learned what it takes to make a marriage work. Forgiveness ranks high up on that list!

For some reason, most of our arguments seemed to start in the car and usually on the way to or from the church. Imagine that! With five small children in the car, no wonder we were on edge! In the middle of an argument, I'd often set a focal point for it to stop. I'd say, "Okay, do you see that billboard down the road? When we get there, we're going to stop this and start laughing." And we would. Of course, our laughter was forced at first, so we felt silly. But that would make us laugh even harder, and we'd forget about why we were ever arguing in the first place!

Laughter is really what ended many of our petty disagreements. One day when all the children were in school, John and I got really frustrated with each other. So he was giving me the silent treatment as he usually did when we argued, because he knew that's what annoyed me the most. I kept trying to get him to talk to me, and he just kept ignoring me. Finally I got so tired of it that I went into Joel's room and hid from him.

After a few minutes, John came down the hall on the way back to our bedroom to look for me. He kept yelling out, "Where did Dodie go? Has the rapture happened, and I'm still here?"

When he walked past me, I jumped out of the room, hopped up on his back, and cried out, "Now I'm not getting off your back until you talk to me and tell me you're sorry!" Pretty soon we both started laughing and totally forgot what we were mad about.

Another time, John got upset with me on the way to church. This time it was about the children. April was acting up, so he stopped the station wagon to discipline her. But every time he'd go to the back to get her, she would rush to the front seat and he would miss her. They just kept going back and forth, back and forth. I thought it was so funny that

I couldn't help but laugh. But John didn't think it was the least bit funny! He got angry with me, and pretty soon he was ignoring me again.

By the time we got to church, John was flustered. Once we got up on the platform together, he realized that he had forgotten the man's name whom he was about to address from the pulpit, so he whispered to me and asked me what it was.

I whispered back, "I won't tell you until you tell me you're sorry!"

He whispered a little louder the second time. "Dodie, tell me what that man's name is!"

I repeated, "Not until you tell me you're sorry!" I did this in the middle of the service on the platform! I was a little character! (I still am! Ask my children.)

Finally John told me he was sorry, and I told him the man's name. He thought it was funny, but not until the next day! We laughed about it for years after that.

These are all examples of petty disagreements, but sometimes couples encounter serious issues that require forgiveness. John and I had some of these as well. So early on, we decided on two things. The first was that we would only argue "from the neck up," not allowing the aggravation to settle in our hearts.

No matter how much you love someone, it's still easy to get disgusted and disheartened with them, especially when you live with them! That's why we must always be kinder than we feel like being. After all, we are to be imitators of Jesus, even toward our spouses. We should be lenient with them, never allowing resentment to enter into our hearts.

Second, we decided to follow the Bible's instructions to never let the sun go down while you are angry (Ephesians 4:26) and to never go to bed angry at each other. I can't tell you how many times John rushed home from work because it was almost sundown on the days when we had been arguing. He took that verse seriously, and I was glad, because when you go to sleep angry, you wake up angry! With true forgiveness, every day truly feels like a new day. If you and your spouse disagree a lot, consider setting these two rules. They helped us tremendously!

> In your marriage, follow the Bible's instructions to never let the sun go down while you are angry.
>
> ~§@ @/~

SPUR EACH OTHER ON

I have never particularly enjoyed speaking in front of people. When John and I used to go on the platform together, I would get so nervous. Sometimes we'd be filming for television, and I'd get my words mixed up. But John would just smile, the people would clap, and we would keep trying until I got it right. He was so patient, and his support always meant so much to me.

Of course, he was an excellent speaker, so it wasn't hard for me to praise him in that way. Still, I always made it a point to tell him how great he did. We should never assume our spouse knows how wonderful we think they are; we should always make it obvious! Healthy relationships require encouragement.

> We should never assume our spouse knows how wonderful we think they are; we should always make it obvious! Healthy relationships require encouragement.

In some situations, our support is even more effective when it goes beyond words. There are times when it is better to *show* our spouses that we believe in them. John was so good at this. He was always there to encourage me, especially in my role as a mother. I was a young mom, so I felt I needed that encouragement often!

There were times when I would get so exhausted, raising and taking care of five children. When John would see me getting overwhelmed, he would help take the burden off. He'd load the children up in the car and take them out for a ride while I rested. Because we didn't have a lot of money at the time, he'd find cheap ways of entertaining them for a few hours.

John loved planes and airports, so he'd take them to Hobby Airport, and they'd go to the observation deck and watch airplanes land and take off. Then they would go to the restaurant and eat apple pie à la mode. They may not have ridden the rides at Disney World, but when the new airport opened, they rode the tram from Terminal A to Terminal B over and over and loved it! People would look at them as though they must be either confused or lost, but they weren't lost; they were having fun. And so was I at home by myself!

When John showed me that he valued me and believed in me, it meant more than it would have coming from any other person. I hope you recognize the potential you have to spur your spouse on. Your words mean a lot to them, and *your* support is what they need most.

Besides praising our spouses, we should also pay attention to how we respond to *their* praise. Sometimes, especially when we are insecure, we don't appreciate it, and eventually they want to stop giving it out altogether. At the beginning of our marriage, I was definitely guilty of this.

Just about every time we would get ready to go somewhere, John would finish getting ready before I would. When I finally finished and walked into the living room, he'd say, "Dodie, you look beautiful." But I was insecure about my flaws, so I would rarely ever say, "Thank you." Instead, I would respond, "John, I know how I look."

One day after having already taken the rejection on lots of occasions, John asked, "Dodie, why don't you just accept my compliment?" I felt badly when I realized what I had been doing. I was letting my own lack of confidence keep me from being thankful for my husband's love for me.

When people say kind things to you, learn to accept it and respond with a kind remark. It would be a dismal world if kind words were never spoken to you, and believe me, there are millions of people in the world who would love to have the ones you refuse! Kind words and sweet responses *can* make or break someone, especially your husband or wife. You can always find something good to say, if you try.

ENJOY EVERY MOMENT

No matter what was going on in our lives at the time, there's one thing John and I always made sure of: We *always* had a good time! We had a date night about once a week. Usually we'd go out to dinner, just the two of us. Once I became a mother, there were times when John had to pull me out of the house, but I was always so glad when he did!

We also went on a few vacations, which are some of my most cherished memories. Our favorite place to go was Steamboat Springs, Colorado, so we'd go there for a few days when he didn't have to preach. I loved it because we didn't have a thing to do but enjoy being together!

If you want a healthy, lasting relationship with your spouse, I encourage you to make having fun with them a priority. Set aside time to spend together. Life gets so busy that if you don't schedule time and hold each other to it, your relationship will suffer no matter how good your intentions.

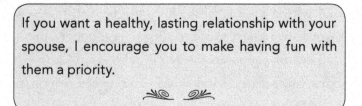

If you want a healthy, lasting relationship with your spouse, I encourage you to make having fun with them a priority.

If you feel badly about leaving your children at home, consider the impact the quality of your relationship with your spouse has on your children. I'm sure if they were older, they would gladly trade a few hours a week with you for your marriage relationship to be healthy. So make time to keep your relationship with your spouse strong and secure. It's not selfish; it's necessary if you want to build a good home!

THE GREATEST IS LOVE

Of all the elements of a successful marriage, love is the most essential, because it includes many things. Where there is genuine love, there will be trust, respect, peace, and so much more. The apostle Paul says, "Beyond all these things put on *love, which is the perfect bond of unity*" (Colossians 3:14 NASB, emphasis mine). In order to have unity in our marriage, love must be shown consistently and unconditionally. In fact, we should go overboard in showing love to our spouse, even in the simplest ways.

One of my least favorite chores has always been unloading the dishwasher. One time John heard me complain about how much I disliked doing it. From then on, as soon as he heard the dishwasher shut off, he'd run and unload it for me. Then anytime I heard him mention that he wanted some apple pie, I would rush into the kitchen and start making one. We did our best to prove our love by serving each other.

I also used to make it a point to remind John how much the children and I missed him when he was on the road preaching at different churches and conventions. I noticed how lonely he would be when traveling alone, so I would write little notes for him and hide them in his luggage. That was such a simple act, but he loved it. We should always work hard to pay attention to each other's needs and feelings. Doing that makes relationships so much stronger.

Not long ago a good friend told me about a dream she had. At the time that she had this dream, she was approaching her twenty-fifth wedding anniversary. With both her and her husband working and raising two sons, things had gotten sort of mundane and routine in their relationship. She and her husband loved God and would never have thought of breaking their wedding vows, but one night she had a dream that disturbed her.

In her dream, she saw herself with another man who was

not her husband. She would meet him on different occasions for dinner or other things. She didn't see his face, and she was puzzled about who he was. On one of the dates he asked her to come to his house, and she agreed. As she drove up to his house, she was feeling an excitement she hadn't felt in a long time. She walked up to the door, rang the doorbell with anticipation, and was stunned when the door opened and there stood her husband!

All that time she had been having an affair with her own husband. God used that dream to help my friend remember how she used to feel and act when they were first married. She was always excited to see him and loved spending time with him. She told her husband about the dream, and they both cried. It was a turning point for her and brought a renewed love and passion into their relationship.

Neither my friend nor her husband had any idea that not too long after she had the dream, he would be diagnosed with cancer. Thankfully, because they had been working on being attentive to each other's needs, they were able to face that difficult time together as an even stronger couple than before. My friend was able to love her husband through his sickness, and today they are healthy, happy, and still extremely observant of each other and very much in love.

Have you gotten complacent with your mate? If so, I urge you to make a change. I always tell wives to kiss their husbands a lot at home, so they won't be tempted by others!

JOINT HEIRS OF THE GRACE OF LIFE

The Bible gives unique instructions for how both the husband and wife are to treat each other. In Ephesians, it says, "Wives, submit yourselves to your own husbands as you do to the Lord" (Ephesians 5:22 NIV). Then it goes on to say, "Husbands, love your wives, just as Christ loved the church and gave himself up for her" (Ephesians 5:25 NIV). A wife is called to submit to her husband's leadership, and a husband is called to love his wife unconditionally.

I have seen wives who were so controlling that I honestly wondered how their husbands could stand them! That's not what God wants. He wants us to respect our husbands as the spiritual head of our homes. In our marriage, John always respected me as well and asked for my advice. We made most decisions together, but when we disagreed, I trusted John's decision. Now, if your husband doesn't serve God, that is another story, and you must honor God's commands over your husband's desires. But as much as you can, live at peace with him and respect him as your husband.

If you aren't yet married, I hope you recognize the importance of finding a godly spouse, one who will assume the role as the spiritual head of your home. From experience, I can tell you that there is nothing more comforting than knowing you can trust your spouse to lead you and your family down the right path!

It only takes a short time as a married couple before you begin to realize that marriage really is a team effort. The apostle Peter calls a husband and wife "fellow" heirs of the grace of life (1 Peter 3:7 AMP). I love that! When we work together, marriage is so much more fulfilling.

I can honestly say that an understanding of this truth is one of the reasons our marriage was successful. We both understood that God had called us to work through any problems *together*, as we loved and respected each other. As John used to say, he was the head of the house, but I was the neck that turned the head!

At times I would try to give John advice, and if he didn't agree, he would remind me that he was the pastor and had to do what he felt best. When things would go wrong in our home, I would remind him, "You are the head of this house so do something about it!" (Bad girl!) We laughed about it.

Marriage is not always easy, but approaching it the way God has instructed us makes it so much easier. Waiting on Him, trusting His timing, and treating our spouse with love causes marriage to be a phenomenal blessing rather than a huge burden.

> Marriage is not always easy, but approaching it the way God has instructed us makes it so much easier.

Life Lesson

Of all the elements of a successful marriage, love is the most essential. Where there is genuine love, there will be trust, respect, peace, and so much more. The apostle Paul says, "Beyond all these things put on love, which is the perfect bond of unity." In order to have unity in our marriage, love must be shown consistently and unconditionally. In fact, we should go overboard in showing love to our spouse, even in the simplest ways.

Chapter 7

Our First Miracle

~❦~

Jesus Christ *is* the same yesterday, today,
and forever.

Hebrews 13:8

When our son Paul was fifteen months old, my husband felt in
his heart that it was time for him to resign from the pastorate
at Central Baptist Church. As a result, John thought he would
be asked to leave his denomination, of which he was on the
board of trustees. He had become somewhat disillusioned with
the fact that almost every time he offered an altar call, many
of the same Christians responded to rededicate their lives to
the Lord again and again. John felt there was something missing, because so many believers didn't have the power to live a
victorious life, but he didn't know what the answer was.

So he accepted a job with a Christian insurance company,

and by the end of the first year he was on the Million Dollar Round Table (MDRT). This was a remarkable accomplishment. Since 1927, the MDRT was the premier association of life insurance–based, financial professionals around the world, an independent association of more than forty-two thousand professionals from four hundred and seventy companies in seventy-one countries. Membership is based on sales and certifications and judged by peers as the best of their best worldwide. I was so proud of him.

As he gained some positive notoriety in the business world, word spread through Houston that he was no longer serving as a pastor and was available to preach on weekends. His phone started ringing and was *always* ringing because John was considered such a master preacher. People really loved to listen to him because he was passionate, loving, and an excellent communicator.

During that period of time, I don't remember a Sunday when John didn't say yes to minister somewhere around Houston. So while he had left his work as a pastor, he never stopped preaching. One day a board member of Hibbard Memorial Baptist Church, which was without a pastor at the time, called him to minister. He preached one Sunday, which turned into a second invitation. They continued to call him back for several weeks in a row and then asked him if he would serve as their interim pastor until they found a permanent one. He agreed, and it wasn't long until they asked him to stay for good. We had already bought a house across town, but the church had a parsonage, so we sold our house and moved there.

We were excited for this journey, but little did we know all it would hold!

MORE ON THE MENU

Everyone at Hibbard Memorial loved my husband. He was a fiery preacher who had such a passion for winning souls. I can never remember him ever giving an altar call without people coming and giving their hearts to the Lord. The congregation started growing and packing the facility, so we began the process of building a beautiful new church.

It was during this time at Hibbard that John experienced an awakening in his spirit concerning the book of Acts. He started to intently study what the Bible said about healing, miracles, and speaking in tongues. He hadn't been taught these things in seminary, so it was all very new to him. He had been taught that the baptism in the Holy Spirit as experienced in the book of Acts was not for today and that the day of healing and miracles passed away with the last of the apostles. In fact, one time John decided to preach on the gifts of the Spirit and he was explaining that the gift of healing was our great modern-day physicians and the gift of tongues meant that people learned different languages. As he was preaching, in his heart he could sense that this was not right, but that's all he knew. So he closed his Bible and said, "People, I don't know what I'm talking about!" At least he was honest.

That's when John had started to sense a restlessness in his spirit—a feeling that he was missing something, that there was "more on the menu," so to speak, for him and for the church members. He was troubled about why people would get saved, but then rededicate their lives over and over and over again. He felt that they were lacking power to live out their Christian lives. So he started searching the Word of God for that power, and that search to discover more started with himself. He was desperately hungry for God.

In Baytown, John had become friends with an Assemblies of God pastor in the area. They would get together for fellowship often. John really enjoyed spending time with this man, but he always doubted any stories the pastor told regarding miracles and speaking in other tongues. One day, not yet knowing about John's questioning of the Holy Spirit, the pastor told John the story of a twelve-year-old girl who began to speak in tongues in one of their services. While she was speaking, a visiting minister from Africa approached the pastor and said, "Oh my goodness! She's speaking in my native tongue. She's giving praise to God in my language!"

When John heard that story, something broke in him. He thought, *Maybe this is true. Maybe there is something more. This sounds just like the second chapter of the book of Acts.* So he continued to search and study the Gospels and the book of Acts more intently.

We began attending tent meetings, and pretty soon we were

witnessing great signs, wonders, and miracles for ourselves. It was so different from what we had known, but it was incredibly exciting. Still, though John now believed in the power of miracles and of the Holy Spirit, he hadn't received the baptism in the Holy Spirit with the evidence of that supernatural power and language. He began to desire, seek, and pray for all that God had for him.

RIGHT ON TIME

God's timing is always perfect. It was during this time of intensely seeking God and studying His Word that our second child, a beautiful little baby girl, Lisa, was born. Not long after we brought her home from the hospital, we realized that she was limp. She had no strength to lift her arms or legs or pick up her head. She had no sucking reflexes. It took me about forty-five minutes to get a half ounce of milk down her throat.

The doctors diagnosed Lisa with a birth injury similar to cerebral palsy due to the umbilical cord being wrapped around her neck. We were told that our little girl might never walk or talk. They also said that she may be in a wheelchair for the rest of her life and that we would have to take care of her as long as she was alive. We were devastated, but because of our new understanding of God's healing power, we were not without hope.

Lisa's condition pushed John even further into learning about God's heart to heal. He closed himself into his library; took off his religious, traditional, denominational glasses; and began to read the Bible for himself day after day. He started to see Jesus in the pages of the Bible helping people, healing them, and lifting them up wherever He went. Then he read in Hebrews 13:8 that Jesus Christ is the same yesterday, today, and forever. In his mind, that verse sealed the deal. The truth of God's Word dawned on him that there was no *day of miracles*, but that we serve a *God of miracles*—a God who is interested in *every* area of our lives at this very moment.

> The truth of God's Word dawned on John that there was no *day of miracles*, but that we serve a *God of miracles*—a God who is interested in *every* area of our lives at this very moment.

It was obvious that John and I needed a miracle, so we began to pray for one. Those were some dark days for us as we struggled to believe, but God was so merciful and compassionate. We read His promises to us over and over. We presented our sick baby to God, *knowing* it was His will to heal her. We were no longer double-minded on it. We believed that Lisa had a destiny beyond what the doctors expected.

Days turned into weeks and weeks into months, and nothing happened, but we continued to thank God for His healing power. And then one day in her fifth month, Lisa began to lift her head and move her limbs normally, which she had never done before. Yet another day at seven months, she sat up on her own as if she'd done it over and over again.

We were so thrilled that we took Lisa to her pediatrician, Dr. Molly Stevens, a great woman of God, who confirmed her progress and even gave Lisa the nickname, "The Miracle Girl," because they could not explain the remarkable change.

By the time Lisa was a year old, she was completely well. It might not have happened instantaneously, but praying for her healing built our faith. The miracle worker, Jesus of Nazareth, touched our little girl and made her whole. Today Lisa remains every bit whole, a mighty miracle of God, and one of the finest Bible teachers I have ever heard. Hallelujah!

Lisa's transformation was a life-changing event for her and for us. Her healing inspired John to change the course of his ministry and his life. It solidified our belief in the power of miracles, which would lead to the decision to start Lakewood, the church that believes in miracles. I believe God allows things in life sometimes so He will get the glory.

I'm so thankful that all of God's promises are *yes* and *amen* (2 Corinthians 1:20). The Bible says that we can boldly approach the throne of God with our needs, because He is a loving Father with a heart to help us (Hebrews 4:16). He *wants* us to be well! *God's power is for today!*

God's power is for today!

THE MISSING LINK

After Lisa's healing, John was convinced that he wanted the power of the Holy Spirit working in his life every single day. So one weekend he took a train to minister at a revival meeting at the First Baptist Church of Blytheville, Arkansas. On the way there and on the way back, he prayed and fasted for God to fill him with His Holy Spirit.

When he got home, he still hadn't received it. Finally John got so desperate for a touch from God that he went to a hotel in downtown Houston to pray more. He told me, "I'm going to go to this hotel, and I'm going to receive the baptism of the Holy Spirit. I'm not coming back until I do!"

To be honest, I really didn't understand what he was talking about. I wondered if I'd ever have my husband back! Thank God, I did. He received the baptism in that hotel room. He was so excited to be speaking in tongues as the Spirit gave utterance, as did those in the second chapter of the book of Acts. He finally experienced for himself this gift that held incredible, life-changing power.

I immediately saw a difference in the way John preached. He preached and prayed with a power and authority that he never had before. Others noticed it too. I remember one of our faithful deacons, Curtis Bell, approaching him after church and saying, "Pastor Osteen, I've been praying for you to receive whatever it was you wanted, and I can tell you got it! Now help me get it!"

Well, this was all completely new to John himself, and he had been on a long journey, so he laughingly said, "I'm tired, Curtis. Get it yourself!"

So he did. Curtis began to seek the Lord for himself. I will never forget when he knocked on our door one night at midnight! We were all asleep in bed, so John went to open the door. When he did, there was Curtis holding a can of coffee in one hand and some cookies in the other!

"Curtis," John asked, "do you know what time it is?"

"Yes, I do!" Curtis exclaimed. "I just received the baptism in the Holy Spirit, and it's time to party!"

John laughed and invited him in. That night we had a little "party" while the children slept. Not long after that, I also received my prayer language. It has been a glorious journey. My prayer life has changed dramatically, because when we don't know how to pray, the Holy Spirit makes intercession through us and for us and prays according to the perfect will of God (Romans 8:26–27).

John found the missing link he was searching for. Jesus said, "You shall receive power when the Holy Spirit has come upon you" (Acts 1:8). The Holy Spirit lives and dwells in every person who has received Jesus as their Lord and Savior, but there is more on the menu. There is a separate experience from salvation that immerses you into a supernatural dimension of prayer, compassion, power, and miracles. It is "to you and to your children, and to all who are afar off, as many as the Lord our God will call" (Acts 2:39).

THERE'S MORE FOR YOU

God desires that we do the same good works that Jesus did. When you read the four Gospels in the New Testament, you will find Jesus doing good to people, loving people, healing the sick and brokenhearted, and changing lives with the Gospel. The power that worked in the life of Jesus while He was on this earth is the same power that works in you and me. The Holy Spirit will anoint you to do the works that Jesus did—to touch hurting people in your world.

The Spirit of the Lord is upon *you* just like He was with Jesus, because He has anointed *you* to preach the Gospel to the poor. He has sent *you* to heal the brokenhearted, to proclaim liberty to the captives and recovery of sight to the blind, to set at liberty those who are oppressed, and to proclaim the acceptable year of the Lord (Luke 4:18–19).

As believers, John and I found out that we lacked knowledge in many areas of the Bible. We loved God with all our hearts, but we learned that we were actually closed-minded to some things God had for us. Sometimes we are taught by others who are well-meaning but lack knowledge in certain areas, so we become blinded by the traditions of men. For nineteen years, John had preached the Gospel of salvation, but he found out that there was more on the menu than he ever dreamed.

The prophet Isaiah explains clearly to us the redemptive work of Jesus on the cross. "But [in fact] He has borne our griefs, and He has carried our sorrows *and* pains; yet we [ignorantly] assumed that He was stricken, struck down by God and degraded *and* humiliated [by Him]. But He was wounded for our transgressions, He was crushed for our wickedness [our sin, our injustice, our wrongdoing]; the punishment [required] for our well-being *fell* on Him, and by His stripes (wounds) we are healed" (Isaiah 53:4–5 AMP).

What a marvelous God we serve! He sent His one and only Son to forgive us our sins, erase our guilt, give us peace, heal our sorrows and pains and bodies, and cause us to be whole—spirit, soul, and body.

> God sent His one and only Son to forgive us our sins, erase our guilt, give us peace, heal our sorrows and pains and bodies, and cause us to be whole—spirit, soul, and body.

Think about that!

Healing.

Peace.

Forgiveness.

Freedom from the past.

Freedom from guilt.

Well-being.

Wholeness.

There's more on the menu for you! The writer of Hebrews says it all: "So what makes us think we can escape if we ignore this great salvation that was first announced by the Lord Jesus himself and then delivered to us by those who heard him speak?" (Hebrews 2:3 NLT).

I don't want to ignore any part of this great salvation freely provided simply by the taking. By faith, believe what Jesus said and receive the power of the Holy Spirit. Jesus paid an awfully big price for you and me to enjoy the wonderful blessings of God. So I invite you to come and dine with me at the Master's table!

Life Lesson

The Holy Spirit lives and dwells in every person who has received Jesus as their Lord and Savior, but there is more on the menu than we ever dreamed. There is a separate experience from salvation that immerses you into a supernatural dimension of prayer, compassion, power, and miracles. The Holy Spirit will anoint you to do the works that Jesus did—to touch hurting people and make a difference in your world!

Chapter 8

Beginning to Fly

I will not cause pain without allowing something new to be born . . .

Isaiah 66:9 NCV

John's encounter with the Holy Spirit drastically changed the way he preached. He returned to Hibbard Memorial Baptist Church with an even greater anointing than before. Because the church was denominational, he didn't say anything to the congregation initially about his receiving the baptism. However, people couldn't help but notice that something was different. They noticed that his preaching had become more powerful, though they couldn't figure out why. He seemed more confident, and his speaking was even more inspiring than before. I knew why, but I also knew I couldn't say anything until the time was right.

It wasn't long before people in the congregation began approaching John, asking him to help them "get what he had," as our friend Curtis Bell already had. Now John knew that the time was right. They had seen the fruit working in his life, so maybe now they would understand what he had found. I could tell that it was hard for John to keep this newfound gift to himself those few weeks, and he was so excited when the doors opened up for him to tell people about his baptism in the Holy Spirit.

John told the congregation that God is a miracle worker and that he was praying for miracles to take place in our church. However, that didn't happen immediately, and he cried to the Lord, "Why don't you confirm your Word, Lord?" He read that the disciples "went out and preached everywhere, the Lord working with *them* and confirming the word through the accompanying signs" (Mark 16:20). Then the Lord spoke to his heart, "Son, go out on that platform and preach My Word, and I will confirm My Word. I will stand behind My Word."

Sunday after Sunday, John faithfully preached the Word. The Bible says that faith comes by hearing God's Word over and over, and it was taking root in the hearts of many people (Romans 10:17). John also began praying for the sick regularly, and besides Lisa's miracle, two more notable miracles occurred in that church. One was a twelve-year-old girl named Mary. On a Wednesday night, God seemed to give John a special anointing for that evening service. He said as he began to talk about the Jesus of the Bible, it seemed as though He marched right out of the scriptures from the Gospels and stood in our midst.

Faith began to rise. Suddenly he noticed Mary sitting in the front of the church. She had a frozen ankle and her foot didn't function properly. Her ankle was as stiff as steel. John said that something welled up in him like a golden bowl full of love. He didn't think about her being sick or crippled. It was not so much that he was conscious of her being in need of healing. He felt only a supernatural kind of compassion for her. It was that night, without John even laying hands upon her, that suddenly, as Mary looked to Jesus, her ankle instantly became normal. She told us that she heard a pop in her leg when God touched her. It was amazing for all of us to see such astonishing miracles!

SOMETIMES PAIN IS NECESSARY TO MOVE FORWARD

Unfortunately, much of the congregation didn't understand this change in John. Because they hadn't been taught these Bible truths, some were wary of it, just as John had once been. He understood their mind-set. Some people heckled him as he preached, and others spread untrue rumors about us. It caused division between those who were open and those who wanted to stick with tradition. We knew that God didn't call the church to be in chaos or discord, so we prayed that He would help us to handle it all the right way.

As much as we prayed, it was still a difficult time. We didn't want division. We just wanted to serve God completely, with all of our hearts, minds, and souls—and with the power of the Helper, the Holy Spirit, whom Jesus promised us (John 14:26). We wanted to draw others to Christ and to grow together in truth and love.

After a few months of this dissension, a member of the board of our denomination called for a trial regarding our pastorate. They put John on trial for account of heresy. This was a time of mixed emotions for us. On one hand, we were extremely excited about this newly discovered gift of the Spirit, but on the other hand, we were discouraged by others' rejection of it.

Although we knew we were doing the right thing and trusted that God would bless us for our obedience, it was still a tough time. We had poured the last couple of years of our lives into helping this group of people grow in God, and now it seemed as though we were being punished for it. It was hard for me to watch my husband go through so much persecution for doing what he knew in his heart to be right. But sometimes that hurt is a necessary part of God's plan. In the midst of it, we should remember that He always has a purpose waiting for us on the other side of our pain.

We were thankful for that truth. Though we experienced pain from that incident, it ultimately propelled us into doing exactly what God had in mind the whole time. It led us to step out and establish Lakewood Church.

During the trial, we had made up our minds that we would not let bitterness toward this board member settle in our hearts. We decided that whatever happened, we would trust God to lead us forward. We would remain confident that He had our best in mind. John asked me to stay at home during the trial, and I'm glad I did.

In the end, 82 percent of the church members voted for us to stay. Nevertheless, we could see that our staying would cause ongoing strife within the church, so we felt in our hearts that it was time for us to go. When John resigned, ninety other church members followed us, and we moved to an area close by called Lakewood. Thus, Lakewood Church was born.

It was a hard time for me personally because I lost many close friends. They turned their backs on us, but I can understand why. I chose to pray for them and forgive them, and I can tell you that God blessed me with many new friends and I have never looked back!

John said that our experience reminded him of the story of a little bird that was hatched in a cage. That bird did not know anything about life outside of that cage, for he had never been outside. As he grew, he began to notice the appendages on his sides and wondered what they were. One day he learned that his wings would lift up and down. He flapped his wings so fast that he flew into the side of the cage. He did that over and over. Deep inside he heard a little voice saying, "You are not made for a cage." But that was the only life he knew.

Then one day someone mistakenly left the cage door open, and the bird flew out for the first time. Can't you hear that little bird saying, "This is it! I was made for something bigger than a cage!"

It is possible to be in the body of Christ and still be all locked up in doctrines that say miracles have passed away and the days of supernatural direction are over. By the power of the Holy Spirit, the cage had been opened in our lives and we began to fly together. We began learning the great truths of the Word of God and experiencing the abundant, victorious life of Jesus Christ!

A few years ago a pastor from that denomination called and asked me to go to lunch with a friend. I did, and they said they wanted to apologize to me for how we had been treated fifty years ago. How sweet! I told him it was not necessary because we had forgiven all, but that was very considerate of them.

THE FOUNDING OF LAKEWOOD CHURCH

During this season, God taught me an important lesson about how to act in hard times. I learned that if we will be faithful to seek God and obey Him when things are tough, He will be faithful to help us through it. He will reward us with a new beginning even better than that ending.

Lakewood Church was our new beginning, and what a great one it was. Although I am thankful for our time at Hibbard, I am so glad that God gave us a new start, because this new start eventually became a place of new starts not just for us, but also for multitudes of people in Houston and around the world.

Our first service at Lakewood was held on Mother's Day in 1959. At the beginning, we met at the Lakewood shopping center on Mesa Road in a big blow-up tent lent to us by the Full Gospel Businessmen's Fellowship. John spoke for the fellowship all over the world, and they were always good to him.

Not long after that, we moved into an old, dirty, run-down feed store in the same area of northeast Houston and converted it into a little church that could seat 234 people. I remember the spiderwebs and the holes in the floor—because it really was an old livestock feed store where the feed would fall through the cracks. It was an unimpressive little facility, obviously different from the many churches one saw in the neighborhoods in Houston. The chairs didn't match and the pews didn't match, but it was wonderful. There was just such a high level of enthusiasm and excitement. To us, it didn't matter so much where we met. We were just delighted that we had a building! We were excited about the road ahead and extremely grateful for our new beginning.

John's first message there was entitled "No Limits." He wanted everyone in that audience to know that there are no limits to what God can do in the life of anyone totally surrendered to Him. From the very start, Lakewood Church saw the world as their mission field, and John was determined to do things God's way, regardless of what anyone said about him or the church.

> There are no limits to what God can do in the life of anyone totally surrendered to Him.

The Bible encourages us to not despise the day of small beginnings (Zechariah 4:10), and those were our humble roots. I remember how the children helped out and how my parents came and pitched in with their support. We learned early on that when you prove yourself faithful to God in the little things, He will trust you with much. "He who *is* faithful in *what is* least is faithful also in much; and he who is unjust in *what is* least is unjust also in much" (Luke 16:10).

No matter where you are today, God can give you a new beginning. You're never too old, too broken, or too far gone to be forgiven, restored, and used mightily by Him. He makes beautiful what others look past, even an abandoned, old feed store, and if you'll let Him, He will make your future brighter and more beautiful than you ever thought possible.

No matter where you are today, God can give you a new beginning.

Life Lesson

Sometimes hurt is a necessary part of God's plan. In the midst of it, we should remember that He always has a purpose waiting for us on the other side of our pain. If we will be faithful to seek God and obey Him when things are tough, He will be faithful to help us through it.

Chapter 9

From a Feed Store to Feeding Millions

Instead, we will speak the truth in love, growing in every way more and more like Christ, who is the head of his body, the church. He makes the whole body fit together perfectly. As each part does its own special work, it helps the other parts grow, so that the whole body is healthy and growing and full of love.

Ephesians 4:15–16 NLT

At Lakewood, John was able to preach freely on his newfound revelation of healing, miracles, and the baptism of the Holy Spirit. He prayed for the sick, and we saw several miracles take place. We were a small church, but we were excited for all that God was doing! John pastored this wonderful church for about a year, until he felt God calling him to a new realm of ministry: the mission field.

A MISSIONARY'S HEART

One night while the children were young, John had a dream in which our middle daughter, Tamara, and our youngest son, Joel, were drowning in the ocean. He could see them come up to the surface gasping for air, and in between waves they would cry out, "Save me, Daddy! Save me!" John woke up trembling, and God immediately spoke to his heart. He said, "I have children all over the world who are dying. They've never heard about me. They're drowning, and they need to be saved. You have to tell them."

This dream opened John's vision to the millions of people who had never heard about Jesus. It helped to inspire in him a passion for evangelizing the world. After much prayerful consideration, he decided to turn the church over to another pastor so he could travel and preach and teach in other nations. He went all over the world and held huge meetings, preaching the Gospel, praying for the sick, and reaching thousands of souls with the message of Jesus. God gave John such a deep love for the people of India and also put a special place in his heart for the Philippines.

John thought he would continue to travel and preach around the world for the rest of his life, but after about eight years, God called him back to Lakewood. John said he was sitting in a restaurant in the Philippine Islands when God gave him the mandate to return. Instantly he thought, *What? Go back and preach in that little church when I'm preaching to thousands of people here?* But John wanted to obey God, so he packed his bags and returned, only to discover that there had been a failure with the current pastor of Lakewood.

The church people were scattered and hurt by what had happened. John saw that they needed a new pastor quickly, so he immediately offered to resume the position. However, the elders were not so sure. They thought that he traveled too much, and they wanted someone who would be in town all of the time. Basically, in a nice way they told him no. But John knew that Jesus had given him specific orders, so he wasn't going to take no for an answer.

At the next service, he got onto the platform and told the people, "When I was in the Philippine Islands, God spoke to me to return and pastor this church. I'll pastor from the pulpit or I'll pastor from the backseat, but no matter what, I'm going to pastor this church." John was so bold that he made me nervous at times! But as usual, it worked. The elders and the congregation welcomed him back, and this time for good.

Although John left the mission field, he always kept his

missionary's heart. In fact, he believed that his time on the field prepared Lakewood for its next season of solid expansion. He used to tell pastors that there were *3 Ws* that caused Lakewood to grow: genuine *worship*, a focus on preaching the *Word*, and an emphasis on reaching the *world*.

> There were *3 Ws* that caused Lakewood to grow: genuine *worship*, a focus on preaching the *Word*, and an emphasis on reaching the *world*.

John started doing as much as he could to spread the Gospel from where he was. He realized that if he could empower missionaries already living in villages around the world, he could reach many more people than by going to each village himself. So he sent money to help missionaries evangelize unreached people groups.

He sent them his books, audiotapes, and television programs to use as ministry tools in their areas. Of course, John did travel at least twice a year, especially to India. He loved the people and nation of India, and to this day his books and messages are still in circulation there.

John also held annual missionary conferences at our church in which he provided the food and housing and strategized with missionaries about how they could more effectively impact people. He would empower them with materials, prayer, and teaching and then send them back with resources to help them reach their area.

I can't even begin to imagine how many lives were touched through those precious missionaries! Because of John's world vision and missionary heart, numerous people from Lakewood were called to go into nations all over the world.

For the rest of John's time on earth, mission work was a major focus in his life and ministry.

WHAT "THE BIBLE SAYS"

Even though John was excited about being back home at Lakewood, we just couldn't seem to fill up the 234 seats in our church. This frustrated John because he had a big vision, so he asked God to show him how to be more effective.

God spoke to his heart and said, "Son, don't worry about preaching fancy sermons. Just teach people My Word. Explain who they are in Christ and what they can do with Him. Show them that every believer is a minister." This word seemed unusual to John, because it came at a time in which the pastors performed all of the important duties in the church by themselves. But still, he obeyed (Ephesians 4:12).

John told the people, "I am only one person. If you are a believer, you are also a minister. Go out and touch the people around you. Tell them what Jesus has done for you. It doesn't matter who they are—bring them to church and we will love them. We want all people in this church. We want the up and in, the down and out, the drug addicts, the prostitutes... everyone. We want to tell them that God loves them."

He also started to focus less on preparing elaborate sermons and began to simply teach the Bible. That's where his well-known confession came from that Joel and many churches around the world still use today. He would have the people quote this along with him before he spoke:

This is my Bible.
I am what it says I am.
I have what it says I have.
I can do what it says I can do.
Today I will be taught the Word of God.
I boldly confess that my mind is alert and my heart is
   receptive.
I will never be the same.
I am about to receive the incorruptible, indestructible,
   ever-living seed of the Word of God.
I will never be the same.
Never, never, never! I'll never be the same.
In Jesus' Name. Amen.

This confession of the importance of the Word of God in our lives was the driving force in John's life, and he never allowed our family or our congregation to forget it. Regarding everything that relates to our lives, he would always remind us of what "the Bible says."

"ENLARGE THE PLACE OF YOUR TENT"

The congregation at Lakewood was wonderful. They listened to John and did what he asked them to do. They brought people in from all walks of life. That was really the beginning of the explosion of growth that our church experienced. The word got out that there was good Bible teaching at Lakewood, that we prayed for people in every service, and that we believed in miracles.

To our surprise, people began to drive to our church from all over Houston. And in Houston that is a big deal, because our city is large and we have lots of traffic. Still, people would drive anywhere from twenty minutes to an hour to get there. We had always been a community church, but all of a sudden people came from every area of Houston.

This sudden growth was also the beginning of our multicultural attendance, something that was and still is so important to us. We want people to know that their pasts, backgrounds, and cultures make no difference to us. Jesus loves us all the same. His heart is that we all worship together. After all, that is what Heaven is going to be like!

Nondenominational and inclusive of all people, eventually

Lakewood became known as what John referred to as "an oasis of love in a troubled world." It wasn't long after John made these changes that the feed store became too small. We had to start believing God for more property and a new building in which to house the congregation.

During a church service, John once looked outside of our little church that seated 234 people, pointed, and said, "Look out there!" Everybody turned and looked at the wall. Then he said, "There is a Chinese store sitting over there, but I see a church seating one thousand people. I am making plans." And he was! John was always making plans!

Every service we would turn and look and make our confession for a larger church. Visitors who came in would stare at us and say, "You're crazy! You all look at the wall and say, 'We see a new church over there!' "

We made our plans as though God meant it when He said, "Enlarge the place of your tent" (Isaiah 54:2). We saved six thousand dollars, but God put it on John's heart to give the money to Pastor Juarez who had a little church down the road. John was like that. He obeyed God even though we needed the money ourselves. We believed what Philippians 4:19 says: "My God shall supply all your need." We finally raised six thousand dollars, which was only enough to pour the foundation.

One day a friend said to John, "Why don't you build that building out there?"

John shook his head and said, "We have only enough money to pour the foundation."

"So why don't you go ahead and pour that foundation?" the friend challenged him. "Every journey begins with one step."

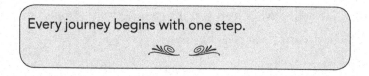

Every journey begins with one step.

He was right. You have to take each step by faith. So we took our seven thousand dollars and poured the foundation for a larger church. When we spent that, more came in, then more and more. God helped us build a sanctuary that seated one thousand people, and we continued to grow and grow.

The day came when we finally got tired of the hard metal seats and upgraded to padded seats. That was a big deal to us back then; we were all excited! We enlarged our auditorium three times before we got to the point where we couldn't enlarge that sanctuary anymore. So in 1987, God blessed us with an eight thousand–seat sanctuary, which we built in the middle of a recession. And even though it cost six million dollars, we paid cash for it.

Just. Another. Miracle.

Isn't that just like God? When we are willing to do things His way, He surprises us in big ways. He is able to do exceedingly and abundantly more than we could ever ask, hope, think, or imagine (Ephesians 3:20). It's easy to get comfortable doing things our way or in the way that it's always been done. When God asks us to change, it's hard to take that step of faith and trust God. But I encourage you from experience to obey God, because His ways are higher than ours (Isaiah 55:9). He will always lead you into a better situation than you could've dreamed up on your own.

AN OASIS OF LOVE

Lakewood continued to grow. People of all races and from all walks of life started to attend. Though our name has changed slightly throughout the years, our goal as a church has always remained the same: to be "an oasis of love in a troubled world." There is no doubt that through God's faithfulness, it has lived up to that goal. We have welcomed everyone through our doors, seeking to love as Jesus would.

Not long ago, I was reminded of what our mission as Christians is to be. I was in one of my favorite Mediterranean restaurants in Houston when I noticed a blind man with a cane sitting and waiting on someone. After a few minutes, three more people came in, two with canes, and one who seemed to have very little sight. I remembered that two of them had come to my healing service on a MetroLift bus a few weeks before.

They ordered their food, and then a server grabbed their trays for them. He turned around, his back facing them. They held on to his shirt and lined up behind him, just as children lining up in school. I cried as I watched them and later walked over to their table to talk with them. They were such beautiful people!

Driving home that day, I thought about how many people are spiritually sightless. I was reminded that just like how that server led those precious blind people to their table, we are called to love those who are spiritually blind and to lead them to Jesus. We must let them know that He died for their sins and sicknesses, no matter what kind of life they have lived.

It is so easy to come to Jesus, but many people make it hard on themselves because their eyes are not opened to His merciful love. If they only knew that He is waiting with His arms wide open. We must be the ones to tell them! Throughout my life, I have strived to adopt Lakewood's motto as my own. I truly want my life to be an oasis of love to all those who are troubled and hurting. Can you imagine how our world would change if we all made this our goal? I think we would be amazed!

REACHING OUT TO MILLIONS

When John returned from the mission field, he still felt in his heart that someday he would preach to millions as he sensed the Lord had shown him when he was saved at the age of seventeen. But year after year, though he felt privileged and grateful for the hundreds of thousands he spoke to at Lakewood, he wondered how that dream would come to pass. In his own mind, he couldn't figure out how it was possible that he could be preaching in Houston every weekend and still be reaching millions around the world.

But one day in the early 1980s, God began to deal with John about the possibility of buying television time and producing a weekly show from our services. This was certainly a time when Isaiah 55:9 couldn't have been truer: "For *as* the heavens are higher than the earth, so are My ways higher than your ways, and My thoughts than your thoughts." It seemed like far beyond where we were at, but again, John obeyed, not knowing if the endeavor would be successful or not, but trusting God fully.

Though all of our children went to Oral Roberts University and loved it, Joel went only one year. He really didn't have it in his heart to go to school in the first place, but he wanted to please us. After a year of studying and working in television production at ORU, he told his daddy in 1982 that he wanted to start a TV ministry at Lakewood instead of going back to school. So after his freshman year, instead of going back to Tulsa, Joel started our television ministry. That was hard for me because I really wanted all the children to finish college, but I learned that God knows what He is doing.

Under Joel's guidance and growing expertise, the Lakewood television program grew beyond anyone's expectations. When John died, he *was* preaching to millions, only not in person! His program and videos went all over the world and were viewed by millions of people. By the end of his life, thousands upon thousands had come to the Lord through his ministry. Still today, lives are being impacted through his work.

Beyond that amazing blessing, when Joel moved home, I didn't know that God wanted to give him seventeen years of schooling under John before he'd become the pastor of Lakewood. Our children's futures are better left in God's hands. He knows them better than we do! He will help them to follow what He puts in their hearts.

John went from a feed store to feeding millions with the Word of God. It didn't happen as he thought, but as always, God's plan was greater! As you pursue God's dreams for your life, don't stress over the "why" or "when." Just work hard and trust that God has a plan to fulfill it in just the right way, at just the right time. As the apostle Paul says, "He who calls you *is* faithful, who also will do *it*" (1 Thessalonians 5:24).

Life Lesson

When we are willing to do things God's way, He surprises us in big ways. He is able to do exceedingly and abundantly more than we could ever ask, hope, think, or imagine. Whatever challenges you may be facing today, always obey God, because He will always lead you into a better situation than you could've dreamed up on your own.

Chapter 10

A Mother's Prayer

The LORD hears his people when they call
to him for help. He rescues them from all
their troubles.

Psalm 34:17 NLT

I really believe that children are life's greatest treasures. They are our most valuable investments on the earth, and the greatest gift that we can leave behind. John and I were blessed with five of these treasures, and each of them brought a special love into our lives.

> Children are life's greatest treasures.

Paul came first. He was our only child for a while. At that time, John was working all during the day, and I was without a car, so after I'd get everything done in the morning, I would spend the rest of the time taking care of Paul. I can remember sitting by his crib while he was sleeping, just watching him and wishing he would wake up. But after I had four more children, I wanted them all to sleep longer!

Paul was my little helper. He was serious, yet so funny. As he got older, he excelled at sports and always worked hard in the summer as a waiter. I remember watching him drive away to Oral Roberts University in his little Spirit of America Vega car that he had worked so hard to buy. Paul became a highly respected surgeon, and still is one!

Lisa was next. She was a sweet little baby and I loved her curly hair. When she got older, she loved to study the Bible, to sew her own clothes, and to take care of her younger siblings. In fact, her youngest sister, April, told me she thought Lisa was her mother growing up! I quickly replied, "Who do you think cooked for you and washed your clothes?" There's an eight-year difference and Lisa did help me a lot with her. Lisa graduated with a degree in business education.

Then came Tamara, the middle child, and the other children called her "Miss Compassion." Everyone loved her. She was like John, always fighting for the underdog. At school she was head cheerleader and class favorite every year as well as homecoming queen. If it was voted for, Tamara won every time! She got a degree in elementary education.

Only eighteen months later, Joel came along as a total surprise to us. (But not to God, of course! In fact, the last two were surprises, but what great surprises they have been!) Joel smiled *all* the time and was very athletic. He was shorter but skilled at basketball and baseball. His nickname was "Peanut" until he grew taller. He became an excellent television producer for our program.

Last, Miss April arrived. She was very similar to Tamara—so athletic and popular, becoming homecoming queen and a cheerleader. She played softball and had a mean pitch! She also ran track. April graduated with a degree in business administration.

You can imagine how busy I was all of those years, always running here and there to Little League games, piano lessons, or cheerleading competitions. You name it, our children did it. Sometimes it was a lot for me to keep up with!

One day I forgot Tamara in kindergarten and her teacher had to take her home with her! That would make the headlines today. Another time, April called home and I was gone. She asked her daddy if he would come pick her up from school, and he said, "Yes, where is it?" You can see which one of us did the running! Regardless of the busyness, each child was precious to us and never gave us one minute's trouble. What a joy to be their mother!

DON'T MISS THE BUS

Mornings were as busy as a beehive for the Osteen tribe growing up. I had five mouths to feed and five children to make the school bus—on time, that is. There were a few mornings they missed the bus, and I had to put them in the car and chase the bus down! I thanked God for the day when Paul and Lisa started driving so they could help out!

My morning routine was the same every day. I am a very routine person and I don't like to get off my schedule. I would get up earlier than the children, prepare breakfast, and make sure they were awake and ready for school with lunch or lunch money in hand. Believe me, that was a full-time job in itself, and I'm glad those days are over and all the children turned out normal! Well, most of them at least!

I remember praying over the children every morning, but not in the detail that they tell me I did. I didn't realize at the time that what I was doing was making an indelible mark on their lives. As I mentioned previously, it is true that our children are little video cameras on legs, because they are recording everything we do.

The children tell me today that the three scriptures that I prayed over them every morning were these:

> *Father, I thank You that the children have Your wisdom and the mind of Christ.* (See 1 Corinthians 2:16; James 1:5)

*I thank You for watching over and protecting them
and giving Your angels charge over them to keep
them in all their ways.* (See Psalm 91:11–12)

Thank You, Father, for giving them favor. (See
Psalm 5:12)

I may have not realized the impact that prayer would
have upon my children, but they are doing the same for
their children. I have nineteen grandchildren and one great-
granddaughter, and I believe that each generation will know
the power of prayer and declaring God's Word over their
lives.

I wasn't the only one who did this. Over the years, John
often preached and taught on the power of our own words.
He was so thrilled that the Bible is filled with powerful statements about who we are in Christ and what belongs to us as
believers. Some of the statements are so amazing that when
we read them, I think we don't really hear them in our spirit.
The promises are so great that even when we do see them, it
just doesn't compute.

John had a wonderful small hardcover book titled *Your
Words Hold a Miracle*. He made it clear that if you want to
change your world, start by changing your words to those
taken straight from the Word of God. For instance, when
you're facing obstacles in your path, you should learn to
boldly say, "Greater is He who is in me than he who is in the

world" (see 1 John 4:4); "No weapon formed against me is going to prosper" (see Isaiah 54:17); and "God always leads me to triumph" (see 2 Corinthians 2:14).

I encourage you to pray the Word of God over your life and your family members. I am talking about speaking out what you want to see happen in your life and their lives. Speak out an abundant future for your children. Whether your child is serving God now or not, just speak out, "As for me and my house, we will serve the LORD" (Joshua 24:15). Faith focuses on a Father in Heaven who changes what is happening now.

In Appendix 2, I've provided you with a list of scriptural declarations for you to use and make your very own. It may seem awkward at first, but if you will faithfully continue to speak God's Word on a daily basis, not only will you be changed, but your circumstances will change. *When you believe God's Word in your heart and speak it with your mouth, God stands behind you to make it real in your life!*

MY SECRET WEAPON

Our children were always good children. I like to believe it was because John and I worked hard to protect them and our home. I was very careful about what I allowed into our home, whether it was the music or the television. I felt it was my responsibility to guard our home environment as David wrote: "I will walk within my house in integrity *and* with a blameless heart. I will set no worthless *or* wicked thing before my eyes...He who practices deceit will not dwell in my house; he who tells lies *and* half-truths will not continue [to remain] in my presence" (Psalm 101:2–7). We established clear boundaries on what the children could do, listen to, and watch.

I also was very careful about the other homes that I allowed my children to enter. If I didn't know the environment of their friend's home, I said no. The children did not always understand my reasoning, but there is so much going on in homes that is contrary to the Word of God, and I wasn't going to say yes just to remain popular. Parents need to know what their children are doing, what they are listening to and watching, who they are with, and to be bold to say no. Do your part to guard the precious lives God has entrusted into your care. Today it is so different with social media that it is even more important than ever.

> Parents need to know what their children are doing, what they are listening to and watching, who they are with, and to be bold to say no.

Another reason that I believe our children were so good is because John and I valued prayer. We saw it as our secret weapon, enabling us to keep our children safe and aware of God no matter how far away we were.

One time, when Paul was eighteen and Lisa was sixteen, John and I went on an overnight trip. Paul and Lisa were very responsible, so we knew we could trust them to watch over the younger children. John explained that they were not to go anywhere, only to do their homework and go to bed early.

At the time, our youth pastors were like family, and they asked April to spend the night with them. Of course, she *really* wanted to go. Lisa told her she couldn't, but Paul thought their daddy would be okay with it, so all of the children took a vote on it. Four out of five voted in favor of April going. Lisa voted against it, but she was overruled! April left with the youth pastors, and later John called to check on them. The children didn't know it, but the Holy Spirit had spoken to him that someone had left the house. So he went down the line, telling each of them good night. When he came to April, they got nervous and tried to hide the fact that she was gone, but it didn't work. They learned a good lesson that night—the Holy Spirit always prevails!

On another occasion, John and I were in India. Paul was in medical school, and the other children were in junior high and high school. My mother and daddy were staying with them, but Lisa was the little mama while I was gone. One day while at track practice, Joel decided to take a shortcut across the football field. When he did, he slipped, fell on a sewer grate, and got a hairline fracture in his knee.

Joel had to be taken to the hospital for surgery. The children handled it well, but they never told us because they knew we would have come home early from the trip. They knew how much their daddy loved India, so they didn't want that to happen. Lisa played the role of Joel's mother, and Paul called and talked to the surgeon. Every morning before school, Tamara would go to the hospital and take Joel clean clothes.

But one day while John was praying, he knew something was wrong. So again, we called home and he asked to talk to all the children. Since Joel was in the hospital, and they hadn't told us, he asked where Joel was. Lisa answered, "He's not here right now. He's gone." That was the truth, but she didn't tell us where he was! When John hung up, he looked at me and said, "There's something wrong with Joel."

So we came home early, and when we got to the airport, the three girls were there to welcome us. John asked where Joel was, and Lisa said, "He's in the car." Well, he was—only he was on crutches! God would often reveal things to John in order to take care of us. I was incredibly blessed to have such an amazing, God-fearing husband to lead our family.

PRAYER KNOWS NO DISTANCE

It doesn't matter how old my children get, I still cover them with prayer every single day, and it still pays off. Now I am praying for my grandchildren and great-granddaughter too. Throughout my life as a pastor's wife and a nurse, I've seen a lot of bad things happen to good people, and for a while this put fear in my heart for my children. One day I prayed to God and asked Him to protect them and to always help me know who to pray for. Since that day, He has answered that prayer again and again.

One time when Paul was in Africa on a medical mission trip during his summer college break, he contracted malaria. There was no way for him to call home and ask for prayer. To this day he says that he was so sick and delirious that he couldn't even pray, but out of his spirit came scripture verses that he had learned over the years, and soon he got completely well. But thank God, one night while Paul was gone, before we had heard anything about his malaria, I dreamed he was a little boy on my shoulders and I was praying for him like he needed help. I even told John about it and began to pray earnestly for Paul.

When Paul returned home, he described to me just how sick he had been but that one day he was healed instantly. We figured out that it was the exact day and time that I was praying! He immediately got out of his bed and continued his mission work there.

Isn't that amazing? Prayer really knows no distance—especially a mother's prayer, I'd like to think!

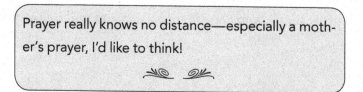

Prayer really knows no distance—especially a mother's prayer, I'd like to think!

Another time, I had a dream that there was a snake slithering in my kitchen, so I called Joel to come over and take care of it for me. When I woke up, I knew that I needed to pray for Joel. That day, as he was driving home from work, it began to rain heavily. As he pulled his car onto the freeway, it hydroplaned, spun out of his control, and crashed into the guardrail. An eighteen-wheeler was heading straight for him, and he says that he thought his life was about to end right there.

But God answers prayer! All of a sudden, Joel looked back up and saw that the semitruck had been moved to another part of the highway. Joel got out of his car and the truck was only three feet away from him. The trucker told Joel that as they were about to collide, a huge gust of wind blew his truck to the other side of the road! He ended with, "I don't know who you are, kid, but you are lucky." We didn't consider it was lucky, but God's grace and protection.

Parents, please never discount the power of your prayers over your children. A mother's and father's prayers are so important. Maybe it won't be a gust of wind that blows your child out of harm's way. Maybe it will be a slower healing like Lisa's. Whatever it is, never give up on prayer. It works! God will always give you the wisdom you need, and your children will grow up to appreciate your prayers and will follow your example.

Life Lesson

Pray and speak the Word of God over your life and your family members, declaring what you want to see happen in your life and their lives. If you will faithfully continue to speak God's Word on a daily basis, not only will you and your family members be changed, but circumstances will change as well. When you believe God's Word in your heart and speak it with your mouth, God stands behind you to make it real!

Chapter 11

Healed of Cancer

O LORD my God, I cried to you for help,
and you restored my health.

Psalm 30:2 NLT

When I wake up, one of the first things I do is thank God that I'm alive. It's not just some routine thing I do; I mean it from the bottom of my heart. There isn't a day that goes by or a special moment that passes that I don't realize: I could've missed out on this.

There could've been a day I'd never seen some of my children married. There could've been a day I'd never met my grandchildren. There could've been a day I'd never seen our congregation move our sanctuary into the former Compaq Center. But thank God, He had other plans.

One day in October 1981, I found myself not feeling quite

like normal. I felt weak and sick, but I was unsure of why. It was nearing the time of our Thanksgiving conference, and I had bought several dresses that I was so excited to wear. But as I was trying them on one morning, I realized that they fit a little more loosely than they did when I had bought them.

I thought at first that maybe I had just been a little stressed with the holidays coming up and the responsibilities for the conference. At the time, John and I already had plans to go to Oral Roberts University in Tulsa, so I didn't say anything about it and decided to go ahead with our plans.

Paul was a medical student there at the time, so we were excited that we would also get to spend some time with him. As soon as Paul saw me, he looked concerned and said, "Mama, you don't look good. You need to go get checked out." I was very jaundiced in my eyes and skin.

I really didn't want to go to the hospital, but after we returned from Tulsa, and at the urging from both Paul and John, I went. I had no strength whatsoever. Even just to get into the hospital bed felt like a chore!

After running a few tests, the doctor told me that he wanted to keep me for a few days. Well, those "few days" went from November 20 until December 10! I was so disappointed that I had to miss the Thanksgiving conference and the usual Thanksgiving festivities with my family. I was thankful for the wonderful doctors and hospital care, but it was the holidays and I just wanted to be home, and my family wanted me home as well.

THE DIAGNOSIS

Finally, on December 10, the doctor met John in the lobby of the hospital. He said, "Pastor, I am sorry about this, but your wife has metastatic cancer of the liver. We can't find the primary tumor."

John came to my room and told me, and I thought, *No way. Not me!*

But there I was at only forty-eight years old, being told that I did, in fact, have cancer. And the doctor's news only got worse. I was given a few weeks to live with or without the use of chemo. What a great Christmas present, huh?

John couldn't believe what he was hearing. He said, "Doctor, I'm going to take my wife home. We are going to pray and seek God, and then we will decide what to do. We believe in miracles, and we believe in the miracle worker."

The doctor said, "Well, Pastor, you're going to have to have a miracle this time."

Paul happened to be in Houston doing an internship at a hospital nearby at the time, so John called him over to hear the diagnosis from the doctor. Paul literally ran the whole way. When he arrived, I heard loud sobs in the hallway. Instantly I could tell that it was my grown son, sobbing like a little boy.

That was a really hard moment for me, for two reasons. First of all, no mother wants to put her family through any pain or sorrow, even if she has no choice. But it was especially hard for me. I prided myself on being healthy and working hard for my family. I can't even count the times I stayed up while everyone was asleep, doing laundry or shampooing the carpets. John often said, "Dodie, it's time for you to stop working now. You've done enough for today."

Second, it was a hard moment because I knew that thanks to his studies, Paul fully understood my medical prognosis just as I did as a nurse. He knew that *only* a miracle would save me.

The doctor wanted me to stay in the hospital, but I was so nauseated and worn out from all the hospital noise and interruptions that I decided to go home. At five o'clock in the afternoon, we all loaded up in Lisa's little car and drove home. April, who was the only child still living at home at this time, saw me when I walked in the house, and she told me much later that she thought I looked like I was ninety years old... in reality, like death.

I didn't realize it, but John had a speaking engagement that night. When we got home, he kissed me good-bye and called a friend to come pick him up and drive him down to Galveston. He went right ahead and preached, even after that terrible news! What an outstanding man he was.

As I sat in my home and thought about my diagnosis, I knew I had a giant of a battle on my hands. How was I going to fight it? As I sat there, something John had told us so many times in church came up in my spirit: "Store up the Word of God in your heart. Then when you need it, you'll have it."

> Store up the Word of God in your heart. Then when you need it, you'll have it.

Well, I needed it all right! I was so thankful then that I had read and studied my Bible for all those years. I knew that God was a God of miracles and that He was my healer.

I began to write out every scripture I knew that spoke about healing. I found two old photos of me in which I looked healthy—one from my wedding day and one of me riding a horse while on vacation in Montana. I posted one on my bed and one on my fridge. I was going to *constantly* remind myself of God's promises to me. (See Appendix 3 for my list of healing scriptures.)

That is such an important lesson to learn. The Bible says that people are destroyed for lack of knowledge (Hosea 4:6). This is sad but so true. Many people don't have knowledge of the Word of God. They don't understand that God wants them healed and whole, and this understanding can be the difference between life and death!

The next morning I asked John to pray with me. He anointed my head with oil, and we lay in our bedroom. John took authority over every cancerous cell in my body and commanded it to leave in the name of Jesus! We proclaimed, as God's Word proclaims, that "by the stripes of Jesus" we are healed (see 1 Peter 2:24).

I also placed my Bible on the floor and slowly put my feet on the Word. It may seem strange, but I physically stood on it and spoke out. "Father, the only thing between death and me is Your Word . . . and I am choosing to stand on it." I believe that is the day when God healed me. However, it took a while for my body to catch on. I still had symptoms and I still felt ill, but in my heart I knew I was healed.

OWNING MY FAITH

During my stay in the hospital, I was so weak and medicated that I relied heavily on my husband's faith and the faith of those who were praying for me, especially the people of Lakewood Church. But when I went home, I knew that it was time for me to rely on my own faith. This was between Jesus and me now.

I realized this when one night, God spoke to my heart so clearly. He said, "Dodie, it's not your husband's faith that will make you well. It is your faith that you must go on now." From that day on, I did my best to build *my faith* every single day.

One of the ways I did this was by acting as if I was healed. Now, this doesn't mean I did anything risky or against the doctor's orders, but I did my best to live my life as if God had already healed me. I only got in bed during normal sleeping hours. I did all of the normal household chores that I could, and I never stopped envisioning myself healed and whole.

During this time, our youngest daughter, April, was still in high school. She often tells the story of waking up one morning to the smell of breakfast cooking. She thought it was her dad in the kitchen (that would've been a miracle in itself!) but ran to find me, swallowed up in one of my dresses, standing over the stove, cooking her breakfast.

"Mama, what are you doing?" she asked, obviously concerned. "You need to be in bed."

"April, I'm not going to act sick," I said firmly to her. "If I'm going to be well, I need to act like it."

"Faith is the substance of things hoped for, the evidence of things not yet seen" (Hebrews 11:1). Sometimes we have to hope when it's hard. We have to act as though we have already received our miracle, living by what we know, not by what we feel.

My dear husband and children were so amazing during this time. Though I am sure they wanted me to rest and to help with the chores, they let me work out my faith. They were supportive and optimistic, even when I'm sure they didn't feel so optimistic. They stood like pillars of strength, never panicking or wavering throughout our battle.

Some days I didn't feel like doing anything but cry. John would see me crying and hurting when nobody else knew it, and he told me over and over, "Sweetheart, you're going to get well. We are going to go all over the world together. We're going to do things for Jesus. Our best days are ahead."

When you are believing for a miracle, it is imperative that

you surround yourself only with those who support you. Having people who will stand with you through every season makes all the difference in the world.

BATTLE OF THE MIND

Still, no matter how strong you are or how solid your support system is, anyone who has been through this type of battle knows what a fight of faith it is. When your mind fights against your heart, and fear fights against all that you know to be true, it can be a battle beyond what you ever imagined.

I was the wife of a pastor, but first of all, I was and am a human being. I had the same thoughts and feelings that anyone else would have had in my situation. I had to work *so* hard to cast down those awful negative thoughts. The Bible tells us to cast down every imagination and take captive every thought that doesn't agree with God's Word (2 Corinthians 10:3–5). And that's exactly what I had to do.

There were many nights when I lay in bed and the devil would taunt me, "You have only a few weeks to live . . . a few weeks to live. See that pink dress in your closet? That's the one you'll wear to your funeral. You look good in it." It was a constant battle of the mind.

During those times, I continued to fight back with God's Word. I spoke it even when I didn't feel like it. I would replace those thoughts with words of faith and say, "With long life I will satisfy him, and show him My salvation" (Psalm 91:16). Hebrews 10:23 became my strength. I would repeat to myself, "Let us hold fast the confession of *our* hope without wavering, for He who promised *is* faithful."

The Word of God would always encourage me and make me feel better, but the enemy challenged every step of faith. However, day by day, my hope strengthened. Day by day, my faith increased, but not without the occasional doubt. When I doubted, I would feel guilty. Was I preventing my healing? That thought concerned me more and more every time I felt fearful or had a negative thought. So one day I approached my husband about it.

"John, what is wrong with me?" I asked. "I feel so condemned because I am wavering."

"Are you wavering in your head or heart?" he asked.

I thought about it for a minute. "No, I know God's Word to be true. He wouldn't lie to me. I'm wavering in my head."

"Then there's no need for you to be condemned," he said sweetly. "Those thoughts are from the enemy. Just resist them in the name of Jesus."

John's words helped me so much that day. They spoke much-needed peace and comfort to my soul.

If you're going through a battle today, accept this fact: In the midst of your battle, you *will* doubt. It's simply part of being human. So please, don't condemn yourself for it; just do your best not to let the wavering move from your head to your heart. And most of all, don't let the enemy torment you!

GIVING AND FORGIVING

There were two more hard but most beneficial things that I chose to do while believing for my healing. One was to continue to give out of my need, and the other was to grant and accept forgiveness.

Even on my sickest days, I attended every church service. John had to pull me up the stairs, because I was so weak. I was also determined that I was going to continue to give to others, because I knew that is what Jesus would want me to do. I distinctly remember the day and moment when I was driving across town to pray for somebody who was sick and I thought, *I probably look sicker than she does!* But I kept going, and I believe God blessed me for that.

I found that when I was alone in the house, I thought about myself, the pain, sickness, and symptoms, and I would get weary and full of pity. Let me tell you: Pity never wins. I always felt better after giving to someone out of my need than I did while having a pity party. It's just as the writer of Proverbs says, "The generous will prosper; those who refresh others will themselves be refreshed" (Proverbs 11:25 NLT).

> I always felt better after giving to someone out of my need than I did while having a pity party. Pity never wins.

The second thing I determined was that I would be at peace with all people. I went the extra mile to make sure everything was right in my heart. One night I woke up and wrote letters to John and the children or anyone I thought I might have offended, asking them for their forgiveness. I had been irritable during those weeks I had been sick. I also prayed to forgive anyone whom I may have held bitterness toward in my heart. I wanted to make sure that nothing I was doing or had done would interfere with God's healing power flowing into me.

After I did these two things, I felt so clean inside. I felt as though I was truly ready to receive not just my healing, but all of the wonderful blessings that God had for me. And boy, has He given me many!

LESSONS LEARNED

Well, those few weeks that the doctor had given me to live are now thirty-five years and counting! God truly worked a miracle and healed my body, and I am forever grateful. Today my greatest passion is to teach people about healing and to pray for those who need healing.

If you need healing in your body, it is important to remember that healing doesn't always come in the same way. Just because I did not use medicine does not mean that you shouldn't. The doctors told me that they didn't think it would help me and that chemo might prolong my life a little. I believe God works through medicine, and I am thankful for doctors who work so hard to help us get well. I believe we should do all we can, and what we cannot do, God will!

It's also important to remember that God is not the one who made you sick and He does not want you to live that way. Did you get that? *It is God's will for you to be well.*

Jesus said it was "the thief," Satan, who came to steal my health, kill me, and destroy me. On the other hand, Jesus said, "I have come that they may have life, and that they may have *it* more abundantly" (John 10:10). You can have abundant life if you want it.

Then we must understand that people's healing comes in different ways. We all have known someone who has believed well and fought hard but has still graduated to Heaven. I don't understand why some of our healing comes as extended life on earth and some comes in the form of dying, but I do know this: God knows what He is doing. As hard as it may be, we have to trust Him during these times and know that He is always doing what is best for us.

That's what I had to do when God chose to take John home. I wanted more than anything for him to be healed just as I had been healed and for him to stay with me, but God had another plan. And I know that His ways and thoughts are always higher than mine.

Finally, please don't ever believe or try to make someone else believe that a person did not live because their faith was too small. This is not the truth! This is the devil trying to torture you with guilt, and it is no way to live.

God wants the best for you and those you love. And only He truly knows what that "best" is.

STILL GOING STRONG

When I was sick, I remembered the amazing story told in Isaiah 38 where King Hezekiah was dying but earnestly prayed and reminded the Lord of his faithfulness. God heard his prayer and saw his tears and added an extra fifteen years to Hezekiah's life. So I reminded God of that. I said, "You gave Hezekiah fifteen years, so will You please give me some extra time. Give me twenty-five or thirty years, please."

Well, a few years ago it dawned on me that my thirty years were coming to an end! So I said, "Jesus, can we renegotiate? At the least, I want to live into my nineties in good health and then go to Heaven well—and in my sleep."

Of course, I'm joking. I want to stay around for as long as God will let me, but I will be happy when He decides to call me home. Until then, I'll keep doing what He has for me to do!

God has been so faithful. There are many different ways of healing, but only one healer, and His name is Jesus. He wants His children well. I am eighty-two years old today, and I'm healthy and strong. I owe my health and all I have been and done with this time I've had to Jesus. *Thank God, He is still the God of miracles!*

There are many different ways of healing, but only one healer, and His name is Jesus. He wants His children well.

Life Lesson

If you're going through a battle today, just accept this fact: In the midst of your battle, you *will* doubt. It's simply part of being human. So please, don't condemn yourself for it; just do your best not to let the wavering move from your head to your heart. And most of all, don't let the enemy torment you!

Chapter 12

Christmas Memories

Then the angel said to them, "Do not be afraid, for behold, I bring you good tidings of great joy which will be to all people. For there is born to you this day in the city of David a Savior, who is Christ the Lord."

Luke 2:10–11

Traditions formed a powerful part in our family and have always brought us closer together. Every year as we've celebrated Christmas and Easter, we've seen how our time and commitment to one another builds new memories as well as helps us to remember the past. It gives us the opportunity to put a pause on our very busy lives and bond together, and for the children it was so evident that it deepened their sense of belonging and security in our love.

When it came to Christmas, we enjoyed many of the same traditions most families enjoy. John and I loved to watch as our children would put their sleeping bags around the Christmas tree in the den, where they would sleep the night before Christmas, chattering away and laughing and doing their best to guess what presents they might be opening in the morning. Then they would slowly drift off to sleep and finally all would be silent.

We made sure the children knew that Christmas was about much more than giving gifts. We decided to keep Christmas as our birthday celebration of the baby Jesus. The real Christmas was the first one, when God gave the world the only gift that we all really need. God became one of us, a gift that the Bible says is "indescribable," and we never want to lose that in the hustle and bustle. Paul remembers when he was a little boy that I made a sign that said HAPPY BIRTHDAY, JESUS and put it on the window. It's little things like that that make the best memories.

It's little things that make the best memories.

For us, Christmas means: "For God so loved the world that He gave His only begotten Son, that whoever believes in Him should not perish but have everlasting life" (John 3:16). And our giving of gifts simply reflects on God's giving to us of His Son.

I think that because John grew up so poor that most of the

time he and his brothers and sisters didn't receive any Christmas presents, he took special delight in buying the children's gifts himself. And rather than buy the gifts, hide them, and then declare on Christmas morning that Santa brought the gifts in the night, John would take each of the children shopping, one at a time, so they could help him pick out gifts for me and the other children. Rather than Santa's helpers, they were Daddy's helpers. But he didn't let them carry the packages of what he actually bought, so he kept them in suspense until we opened presents on Christmas morning.

"AHHHAAA-HAAAAAA!"

We did have one Christmas family tradition, however, that I am fairly certain no other family kept. It may sound a bit odd today, but when our children were small, every one of them was a coffee drinker. Back then that was true of a lot of families. What made our coffee drinking different was that John loved coffee, the classic old Folgers "mountain grown, the richest kind of coffee." He made an event out of drinking his first cup in the morning, and the children loved it.

So on Christmas morning, the children would get up first and brew a pot of coffee. Then they would gather around the kitchen table with great anticipation and wait for their daddy to join them. He would make his entrance in his thick terry-cloth bathrobe and house slippers, then pour himself a steaming cup of coffee.

John would lift the mug to his mouth, close his eyes, and take a long, slow sip, and then he'd hold the mug up in the air and smile the most delightful smile you've ever seen. That was just the start! The children would sit on the edge of their chairs as John would take a deep breath and hold it; then he let out a sound that would have delighted any marketing and sales executives at Folgers. "Ahhhaaa-haaaaaa!" It was perfect.

All of the children would laugh almost hysterically, and then they would take a sip of their cups and join together in one mighty "Ahhhaaa-haaaaaa!" It was a wonderful scene that I never tired of watching.

In truth, John performed this same ritual every morning after his first sip of coffee. And the children laughed every time they were there to witness it. It wouldn't surprise me that all of our children, and even some of the grandchildren, make the same sound after their first sip of coffee each day.

SWALLOWED UP BY PLUSH PILLOWS

Another Christmas tradition we enjoyed together was a big dinner with my parents. Granddaddy and Grandmama Pilgrim were such a rich source of love and support for all of our children. They didn't just come and stay with us at

Christmas, but they would come several times a year, and the children loved having them. Whenever John and I would go on a church mission or a vacation, they would stay with the children.

My mother would cook the most wonderful meals, and my father would mow the yard and fix things around the house and take Paul hunting and fishing. As good as my mother's pecan, pumpkin, and mincemeat pies were, our children will tell you that they loved her hugs even more. Paul says being hugged by her was like being swallowed up by plush pillows!

But more important, they would share with the children stories from their lives. It helped the children come to know who they really were and all that had shaped their lives. It is something every grandparent should strive to do, and I encourage you to share your life with your grandchildren. You can help them avoid some of the mistakes you made as well as discover what God has taught you. Your love can make all the difference in the world in their lives.

THE GIFT OF FAITH

We did have a couple of Christmases that didn't quite measure up to the others. One year John didn't make it home for Christmas, which came as a shock to us all. He was in India on a mission trip and missed his return flight. I can tell you that there were some very sad faces at our house on that Christmas morning. I did my best to make it fun for the children, but there was no replacing their daddy's absence on Christmas morning, and I missed him too. He was gone for thirty-seven days on that trip.

As disappointing as that was, it taught the children that there are many people in the world who have never experienced anything even close to the love of our family. They realized how other people sometimes feel lonely and lost over the holidays. And it was an easy reminder that on that very first Christmas Day, Joseph and Mary probably didn't have it so wonderful in the manger as a birthplace. In different ways, we all realized the importance of family that year.

Another Christmas that was even more difficult was in 1981, right after I had been diagnosed with liver cancer. I was only forty-eight years old, and the cancer diagnosis came two weeks before Christmas. April was our only child still at home at the time, so as the other children arrived home for Christmas, they had to confront the reality of the cancer and the few weeks I'd been told I would still be alive and with them.

I so wanted it to be a regular Christmas, but I weighed only eighty-nine pounds and I felt terrible. John told the children that they had to trust in God and stand fast and pray with me for a miracle, and they did. They did their best to cheer me up with lots of teasing and laughter.

I didn't know that before the doctor's terminal diagnosis, the children had been planning to give me a beautiful china set for Christmas. Rather than cancel their plans, they decided to go ahead. Lisa especially felt that the china would assure me that they believed I would be healed and be with them for many more family dinners and holidays.

On Christmas Day, I wasn't feeling well, but I kept on smiling and gave everyone long hugs. I was overwhelmed and so grateful when I opened the china set, but when Lisa told me that it would take a month or so before all the pieces of the set were delivered, it caught me off guard a bit. The thought immediately arose *I might not be here that long*. In truth, that entire Christmas season I felt I was in a constant spiritual battle to keep a grip on my hope for healing.

Christmas 1981 was a rough one for me and for the entire family, although going through it brought us even closer together. But the china set helped set the tone for the fight I was engaged in, a gift of faith that helped empower me. I still have that china in my cabinet, and it's a lovely reminder of the power of my family's faith and love. When I cook a dinner (which is very seldom!) and we sit down to the table with those plates, cups, and saucers, I am so grateful for another chance to enjoy all that we have together.

Always be grateful for the time you have with your family members, and not just over the holidays. Make the most of every day, every moment, and bless the Lord for His continued blessings.

A MILLION LAUGHS... AND COUNTING

Whatever your family traditions, whether for a holiday or for every day, remember to make them fun. John was so good at filling our family times with laughter. When he was seventy-five years old, he still laughed and kidded as though he was twenty. He was so responsible and serious, but he also knew how to have fun.

Joel likes to tell the story of the time he and his father were walking down the main street in a little town in Mexico when an American family approached them.

The man asked John, "Do you know where the post office is?"

John gave them a strange look and said, *"No comprende. Español, amigo?"*

They shook their head no and the man spoke louder. "Post office."

Blank look. *"No comprende."*

A bit exasperated, the tourist spoke even more emphatically. "Post office! Mail a letter!"

John's face lit up and he asked, "Post off*eece*?"

"Yes! Yes!" the man exclaimed. "Post off*eece!*"

Then John smiled and replied, "It's right around the corner."

The man burst out laughing and said, "Boy, I ought to whoop you."

But it was also true that sometimes the tables could be turned on John. My daughter April likes to remind me of another time when John decided it would be good and appropriate that we sit all the children down and have a family devotional time. That meant gathering five children around the table, facing one another, with John and me at opposite ends of the table. He pulled out a large blue book with a picture of Jesus on the front of it and began to read.

Things started out well enough with all five children sitting, quietly listening, but before too long, one would catch the eye of another and begin making faces. The others would smile and desperately try to hold back from bursting out in laughter.

I saw them all trying to hold back the laughter, but inevitably one of them would finally break out laughing so hard. And believe it or not, oftentimes it was me. It was just too funny. And when I did it, John couldn't possibly correct the children's behavior, and before long he'd give in and join in the laughter. That tradition didn't last very long! John got disgusted!

We decided to give each of our children their own Bible to read each day. We told them to read it as if God were speaking to them and mark the scriptures that God uses to speak to them. Each of our children is strong in knowing the Word of God, and all of them preach and teach and are in the full-time ministry. Hallelujah!

Jesus said He came to give us an abundant life, and we found great joy in our family traditions and a million laughs . . . and counting!

Life Lesson

We decided to keep Christmas as our birthday celebration of the baby Jesus. The real Christmas was the first one, when God gave the world the only gift that we all really need. God became one of us, a gift that the apostle Paul said was "indescribable," and we never want to lose that in the hustle and bustle.

Chapter 13

The Gray Box

And this same God who takes care of me will
supply all your needs from his glorious riches,
which have been given to us in Christ Jesus.

Philippians 4:19 NLT

By now I've given you quite a bit of background about John
and what made him the pastor he became. Now I want to tell
you more about him as a man, as the love of my life, and as
the amazing father of six children. He was a great man, and
he changed my life forever.

John Hilary Osteen was born in Paris, Texas, on August
21, 1921, to Willis Jackson and Ellen Mae Leigh Osteen.
They were wonderful parents who were cotton farmers. As
was true of an estimated 750,000 farmers during the Great
Depression, they lost virtually everything, including their

farm. They moved to Fort Worth, Texas, where they raised three boys and three girls.

In Fort Worth, John's daddy began going door-to-door selling vegetables, and John would often help him. They also worked out in the fields. John's mother worked in a Laundromat for ten cents an hour. John and his siblings grew up extremely poor. In high school, he would usually have only a biscuit and water for lunch, and many years their family was given the Christmas basket donated for the needy families. Sometimes they didn't even have enough milk for their cereal. They would use water instead. John used to talk about going to school with holes in his shoes because he only had one pair.

He didn't make very good grades in school, so he dropped out of high school and got a job selling popcorn at a theater, which is still there today. It was during this time that John made the decision that changed his life forever—he gave his life to Jesus. From that moment on, he worked hard to become the man of God that he was, and something rose up inside of him—a faith, a boldness. He searched the scriptures to see what God said about him and started seeing himself not as a farmer's child with no future, but as a child of the Most High God. He was determined that his children would never experience the poverty he endured, that no generational issue from his past would end up affecting his children or grandchildren. He was determined to leave behind a legacy of integrity, compassion, and vision.

It didn't happen overnight. After John and I married, there was a period of time when we struggled to pay our bills. One time, before we had children, we only had enough money to buy one sandwich. We bought it, divided the sandwich, and ate it. We would always give God our tithe, which is the first tenth of our income, but we began to learn about how God wanted to bless us in the financial area. Many times we would give offerings to missionaries or give to the church sacrificially, and God was faithful to provide for our needs.

John decided that we would always pay cash for everything except our home, so we would not be in debt. That made us budget our money wisely, and it has paid off. He did the same with Lakewood, and he left the church in good financial order when he went to Heaven. One of the things he taught people was to give 10 percent to the Lord, save 10 percent, and live on the 80 percent of their income, only going into debt for their home and, if necessary, their car. This principle worked well for many others and us.

So many pastors looked to John as their pastor, and he would often have conferences with pastors and ministers only. One thing he taught them was to *live off the top of the barrel*, which meant to fill their barrel up once and live off of the reserve. In other words, don't get their church into debt, but pay cash for everything and be wise to maintain a good reserve for emergencies. He would tell them, "If you can't afford it, wait until you can. Sit on an apple crate until you can afford a chair." He was a very wise man and manager of our money and God's money.

> If you can't afford it, wait until you can. Sit on an apple crate until you can afford a chair.
>
> ✎   ✎

Another lesson that it took both of us some time to learn was to receive God's blessings when they came. When John first started out as a pastor, the church could afford to pay him only a little over a hundred dollars a week. When the children came along, we could hardly make ends meet on that amount of income, but we really didn't expect there could be more.

I remember during a time of special services at the church, we hosted the guest minister in our home for an entire week. We were pleased to do it, though it made us pinch our pennies. The following Sunday a businessman in the church came to John and said, "Pastor, I know things are tight and you've incurred some extra expenses. I want you to have this money to use personally to help out." He then handed John a check for a hundred dollars, which in today's dollars would be worth ten times that amount!

John was stunned by the man's generosity, but he said, "Oh no, brother, I could never receive this money. We will put it in the church offering."

Later John said, "With every step I took as I walked to the front of the church to put that check in the offering, something inside was saying, 'Don't do it. Receive God's blessings. Receive God's goodness.'" But he did anyway, and afterward he said he felt sick about it.

We needed that money, and God was trying to bless and increase us. But John couldn't receive the blessing because he was struggling with a poverty mentality. It took us a while to know that as God's children, we are able to live an abundant life, that it is okay to prosper, and that we should even expect to be blessed. It is as important to learn how to receive a blessing as it is to be willing to give one.

A MAN OF INTEGRITY

From the very first time I heard John speak in our church, he was already recognized as a man of great character, and people around him recognized it and spoke about it. As I mentioned previously, even when John went through an unwanted divorce while he was the pastor in Baytown, it was evident how his character upheld him. I was a member there during that time, so I saw the rejection he went through.

Because John lived with integrity during that hard time in his life, God honored him, and He blessed him more than he could have ever imagined. Just as He blessed my husband, He will do the same for all of us. If we will strive to do what is right in God's sight, He will honor us. Jesus is always there for you, in the good times and the difficult times, whether it involves a divorce, a sickness, or an addiction. No matter what, you can count on Him. He is faithful.

This heritage of honor was something John wanted to leave behind for his children more than anything else. He worked hard to be a wonderful father and husband, to show them what kind of a man he was, a man who practiced what he preached. He wasn't a perfect man, but he showed them that their daddy was the same no matter who he was with or what he was doing.

One of the main ways he did this was by listening to and obeying God, no matter who it might have upset, including his wife! One late summer day as we were driving home from church, I mentioned to him that God had put it on my heart to give money to people I saw who were in need. School was about to begin, and I knew there were a lot of single mothers in our church who had no money to purchase school supplies for their children or to take care of their children in college.

I asked John for twenty-five hundred dollars in fifty-dollar and hundred-dollar bills to give out to hurting people. He thought about it for a minute; then he kindly said, "Dodie, if I felt led to, I would give it to you, but I don't feel led to do that right now."

I was crushed. I thought, *How dare he turn me down?* So for a while, I went through the house calling him "Stingy Gut." I wouldn't let the children say the word *gut*, because I didn't think it sounded nice, so I said it when they weren't around. I was a little rascal! He never budged, but he did laugh every time I said anything about it.

A few days later, a man in our church called to ask if he could come by our house and talk to John. I told the man to come over because he was home. When he got there, I left them in the living room to talk. A few minutes later, John screamed, "Dodie, come in here!" He asked the man to tell me what he had told him.

This precious man told me that God had spoken to his heart to "go to the Osteen home, give Dodie twenty-five hundred dollars in fifty-dollar and hundred-dollar bills, and ask that it would specifically be given to people in need." Can you believe that? It was the very thing I had told my husband in the car! You would have thought that man had been sitting in the backseat of the car when I said it to John.

You can imagine how I felt once the man left. I knew I had to repent for how I'd treated John. He was not a "Stingy Gut"; he was a wise man who followed what he sensed God was showing him. God had another plan to provide this money for me to give out to others. This is just one example of John's devotion to listening to and obeying God. His commitment spoke volumes to me throughout all of the years that we were together.

As I began giving the money out, I asked each person to write a thank-you note, and I sent them to the man who gave the money. It was a gift that made so many people happy! God knew what He was doing in that situation, just as He always does. In fact, I am still reaping the effects of my husband's obedience that day!

Since that time, four different people have asked me to distribute large amounts of money to people with specific needs. Two of the donors live in other cities, one in Houston, and one is the father of a man whose funeral I conducted some years ago. He gave it specifically for people who needed help paying for funerals.

One of my greatest joys is mailing thank-you notes from the people who received the help to the ones who have so generously blessed them. I have been overwhelmed at the goodness of God. When we choose to follow God's voice, no matter what others say, we will reap the rewards for years to come.

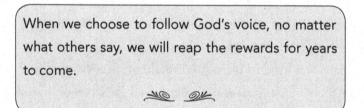

When we choose to follow God's voice, no matter what others say, we will reap the rewards for years to come.

A MAN OF COMPASSION

John was a man of compassion who carried in his big heart a great love for people. So many people looked to him as a father figure and a mentor, because he nurtured them and treated them with love and respect no matter where they came from or what they looked like. I am still reminded of this often to this day.

Several years ago, I took an elderly couple out to eat for their anniversary. When I asked for the check, the waitress told me that she and the waitstaff were treating us. Then she told me her story. She said that she moved to Houston from another country in 1987. Her husband had brought her here and then divorced her. She had no job or family here, so she got a job at an Austrian restaurant, one of my favorites.

One day John went to eat lunch at that little restaurant. As he was leaving, he randomly walked up to her, slipped something into her hand, and said, "This is for you." When she looked, she saw that it was a hundred-dollar bill. She asked him if he needed change, and he said, "No, it's for you." She didn't even know who he was, so she asked the owner. His reply was, "That's Pastor John Osteen. You'll be hearing a lot from him."

That's the kind of impact he made on people, the kind you don't forget. After all those years, that lady remembered the compassion he had for her. I'm sure John knew nothing about her circumstances, but he just followed God's still small voice. Wouldn't it be wonderful if all of us lived like that?

That's just one of the many stories I have heard over the past fifteen years. I can only imagine how many people this wonderful man touched in his lifetime. And every day I am more in awe of how many lives he continues to inspire, including his own children and grandchildren.

A MAN OF VISION

Once we had children, John determined that any unhealthy generational issue from his past would not affect his future or the future of his children or grandchildren. One of these was a fear of lack.

Because John was raised in the Great Depression, he had to overcome a poverty mind-set. He never wanted his children to live under that kind of bondage. He taught them to be wise with their money and to never be afraid of not having enough. From telling stories of God's faithfulness to teaching the children scripture verses, there were several ways John did this.

One of my favorites was the Gray Box, an infamous object in our household and now also in the households of our children. The Gray Box was a metal box that we kept cash in so that when the children needed money for lunch, a football game, a class trip, or whatever it was, they could just go by and get whatever they needed without even asking us. It basically served as our private little Osteen family bank.

I still have the Gray Box, and it's amazing that the hinges on the lid did not wear out through its constant use. The children never took too much and were never dishonest. We always kept the Gray Box replenished for them—there was never more than thirty or forty dollars in it, usually half of it in change and the rest in small bills. We wanted to show them that just as their earthly father and mother always would provide for them, so would their heavenly Father. It created a sense of abundance for the children, a feeling that there always would be enough for all to share in and that they would always be taken care of.

Years later, after all the children were married and had children, John asked me to go out and get a gray box for each of them. I went out to get some, but they were seventy-five dollars each. I came home and told him I wasn't going to pay that much money for a plain gray box. (Who was "Miss Stingy Gut" now?)

Not long before he went to Heaven, John mentioned the gray boxes again. I felt a real urgency to get them this time, so I went out and found some for nineteen dollars each! We put money in them and gave one to each couple for Christmas. I wrote a really sweet note to put in each one, and we were so thrilled to give it to them. Less than a month later, my beloved went to Heaven. The children were so touched by those gray boxes, and they certainly have done their jobs.

Today that fear of poverty is completely broken in our family, and I know without a doubt it is because of my husband's vision for the future and his commitment to breaking any kind of stronghold that could've taken root in our lives and children and the generations to come. I am so grateful!

Life Lesson

Teach your children to be wise with their money, always give 10 percent to the Lord, and never be afraid of not having enough. From telling stories of God's faithfulness to teaching the children scripture verses, show them that just as their earthly father and mother always provide for them, so will their heavenly Father.

Chapter 14

God's Got You Covered

That is why I tell you not to worry about
everyday life—whether you have enough
food and drink, or enough clothes to wear.
Isn't life more than food, and your body
more than clothing? Look at the birds.
They don't plant or harvest or store food
in barns, for your heavenly Father feeds
them. And aren't you far more valuable to
him than they are?

Matthew 6:25–26 NLT

When we think of miracles, we tend to think of church services or large meetings where prayer for healing is the focus.
But miracles are for the home as well, for the most basic
needs in our daily lives, for what some people would consider

the insignificant things. I prayed over just about everything, whether it was a broken washing machine, a broken lawn mower, or for a new dishwasher.

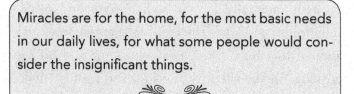

Miracles are for the home, for the most basic needs in our daily lives, for what some people would consider the insignificant things.

One summer I asked God for something that might seem insignificant to other people. It was when the children were in school, and I decided that I wanted a swimming pool in our yard instead of paying for them to swim in the neighborhood subdivision pool. I talked to John about it, and he said a pool was too expensive, and he didn't want to have one built. So Miss Nagger started in again, walking around calling him "Stingy Gut." Be careful of that! No one likes to be called that, and the Bible speaks against nagging. I caught myself doing it often. It was something I was always working on.

Well, John stood his ground. Time went on, and the week of our big annual conference came. We would invite missionaries from all over to come to this conference and rest. At that time we had cottages on the grounds, so people who were serving God could come, stay, and get refreshed. One day during the conference, we saw a beautiful mobile home on the grounds. So we went to visit the couple, Pastor Richard Sarver and his beautiful wife, Dot, and their son, Randall.

Randall had encephalitis when he was a child, which affected him mentally. He was so handsome and lovable. We prayed for him and loved the family the entire week. Richard mentioned that he worked as a contractor and built swimming pools on the side. My ears perked up big time! But I didn't say a word.

After the conference was over and everyone went home, we received a call from Richard. He said God had put it on his heart to build us a swimming pool! Can you imagine how I felt? Jesus took care of me again! And in a way that could have seemed so insignificant to someone else, but not me.

So one week, while our family was out of town, Richard brought a crew to our home and built us the most gorgeous pool. It was far beyond what I could have imagined. To think that God would lay it on his heart to do that for me. I was so blessed! We loved that pool so much.

When it was finished, the children and I put on our swimsuits and started out to swim. John put his swimsuit on and came out the back door. When I saw him, I said, "Don't you dare get in my pool! I believed God for this, not you!" Of course, I was joking with him, and we all laughed. Our family enjoyed that pool for years! Every day it reminded me that nothing is too big or too small for God.

"LIKE A CHOO-CHOO TRAIN"

When the children were young, John traveled to other cities as well as went overseas for ministry work, often for weeks at a time. I stayed home to take care of our five children by myself. When John was away on these long trips, invariably a couple of the children would either get sick or have some kind of accident that made it even harder on me.

It seemed as though these little illnesses always occurred when John was away preaching and praying for the sick. It got so I began to be apprehensive about him leaving. If he had a trip planned, it seemed symptoms of colds or fevers would arise about the time he started packing his bags. There were times when I thought, *Oh boy, here we go again.*

John finally got fed up with all the sickness. He said, "God, I'm going away to do Your work, to help people, and here my own family is falling apart again. It is enough! It is enough! It is enough! I am not going to allow this anymore. I am through with this sickness in the name of Jesus!"

First, John gathered our entire family together. We prayed in every room of our house and decreed that the blood of Jesus prevailed in our home. But he wasn't finished. Instead of just praying over us, he asked all of the children to come outside to the backyard. They were eleven years old and under. He lined them up from the oldest to the youngest, with John in the front, and they had to grab the shoulders of the person in front of them. Then he led them "like a choo-choo train," as Joel says, around the perimeter of our property saying, "Father, I want to thank You that no weapon formed against my family will prosper, and You said Your angels will watch over them and no sickness would come near our dwelling."

John had them repeat his words, "No sickness, no disease, and no accidents."

As he led them out to the front yard, making sure they covered every square inch of our property, I'm sure the neighbors looking out the windows thought they were crazy, and I have no doubt that the children cringed a bit when their friends stopped to stare and cars slowed down. I'm glad I stayed in the house! But do you know from that day forward when John went on those long trips, we never got sick again while he was gone!

FROM WARTS TO CARS

Miracles are for the home and the little things that we sometimes don't even consider. When Paul was a little boy, he had warts all over his hands. I tried in every way I knew to treat them so they would go away. Then it dawned on me one day that I could pray for him to be healed. So I laid my hands on him and commanded the life of those warts to leave in the name of Jesus. I believed the Word of God had taken effect, although the warts still could be seen clearly. We looked at them day after day and said in the face of their continued presence, "Paul is healed in the name of Jesus." We rejoiced and praised God that Paul was healed. About two weeks later, Paul came in all excited. Several of the warts had disappeared. Soon all of them were gone!

On another occasion, Lisa had a mole that was bothering her. I commanded that mole to wither and die, and it turned black and fell off in a few days! How practical and real God is in our daily lives!

More recently, our family and some of our staff members were at the airport parking lot late one Friday night. We had just returned from a Night of Hope event with Joel and his wife Victoria in another state. It was one o'clock in the morning, and we were all exhausted. We got to our cars, and I discovered my car battery was dead. The lights had been left on by the person who parked my car.

Paul and Joel went to work with jumper cables, and my car lights came on, but the engine wouldn't turn over at all. It didn't make a sound, so we waited, trying to charge up the battery. Ten minutes later, still not a sound. The engine wouldn't budge. Then a mechanic from the airport came out to help us, but he couldn't make it happen.

It was very cold and rainy that night. After about thirty minutes of trying everything they could think of, Paul said to me, "It won't start. Just ride with me, and we'll come get the car tomorrow."

I looked at Paul and said, "No, I have two funerals tomorrow. I need my car."

Then Joel jumped in and said, "Mother, I'll give you my car for tomorrow. You can drive it home tonight, and Paul will take me home."

I said, "I don't want your car. I want my car. Let's try it again."

They tried again, but still nothing happened.

Joel was getting exasperated with me and said, "Mother, we can stay here all night, but the car is not going to start. We might as well go home."

"Give me the keys," I said.

Lisa was sitting in her car and watching this unfold, and she said to her daughter Catherine, "Just watch because she is going to command her car to start in the name of Jesus, and it will." And that's exactly what I did.

I got in my car and started praying. And all of a sudden, the car cranked right up the first time. I revved that engine good and loud; then I took off and drove around in circles in the parking lot to celebrate at two o'clock in the morning! Then I thought it would be fun to just zoom off and leave them standing there with big smiles on all their faces. O ye of little faith!

When you face situations that seem impossible in your everyday life, God says, "I dare you to pray and ask Me for help." He wants to be good to you. He wants to show you His favor in new ways!

NOTHING IS TOO SMALL

One day when Tamara was about ten, she decided that she wanted a rabbit. I have no idea why, since we seemed to have every other animal imaginable. The children had dogs, chickens, a goat . . . you name it, and they had it. All against my wishes, I might add! Not because I didn't love animals, because I do. I just loved a clean house more! Today every one of my children has at least one dog, which I try to avoid because they are so huge, but they gravitate toward me! April and Tamara have dogs that almost knock me over every time! April has one that weighs ninety pounds!

Regardless of all this, Tamara wanted a rabbit. One afternoon on her way home from school, she saw a little sign nestled in the middle of some trees that read: RABBITS FOR SALE. She asked her daddy if she could go get one, to which he replied, "Honey, we've got a houseful of children. We can't add a rabbit." Tamara didn't miss a beat, responding, "But you say we have a miracle in our mouth, and I want a rabbit." John tried to reason with her, "No, Tamara. We don't have a pen, and they multiply." But she had a plan. She informed her daddy that she'd already talked to her big brother Paul, and he was going to build her a rabbit pen. Still, John said no, but she kept asking.

After a few more rounds, John finally asked, "Tamara, what sign did you see? I didn't see a sign!" She looked at him and confidently said, "Come on! I'll show you." So she told him where it was back along the road, they pulled over, and she led him back into the trees. Sure enough, there it was—a little teeny-tiny sign. John couldn't understand how Tamara had spotted that sign all the way from the road. Because of his little girl's determination, John just couldn't resist. So Paul built the pen, and we got her two rabbits. Tamara was so happy! Soon we had more and more rabbits!

Sometimes that little sign can be just like a promise we have from Jesus. Others might not see it. It may seem small and ordinary, but as we hold on to it and seek it out, it gets bigger and bigger until it is eventually fulfilled.

Whatever you need from God, dare to ask God for it. He is such a good and loving Father who wants to bless you. If it doesn't come as you expected, remember that God's ways are better than our ways, so the outcome will always be for your best. Your heavenly Father would never do you wrong. He wants the best for you!

Whatever you need from God, dare to ask God for it.

IT TAKES A CHILDLIKE FAITH

When others don't see what you see, as Tamara did with the rabbit sign, it takes a special kind of faith to keep holding on. It takes a childlike faith—one that hopes even when there seems to be no reason to hold on. We have to trust our Father completely, not because we know exactly how His plan will unfold, but because we know *Him*. We know that when He gives us something, it is His best.

One day I was taking care of April's son, Garrison, when he asked if he could take his socks and shoes off. I said, "Of course," so he took his little black tennis shoes and plain black socks off, carefully picked the socks up, and looked at them intently. The socks were faded black crew socks and were worn-out, but he knew his parents had bought them for him, so he loved them. I watched him fold his little socks, and then he looked at me and asked, "Isn't they pretty socks, Grandmother?"

Obviously, to any other person, those socks didn't look very nice, but Garrison loved them because they were from his parents. He had complete faith that if they had given them to him, they were the best, even though they didn't look like it. How beautiful it is to see things the way children do. They love without reason and trust completely, seeing the good and fine in others instead of focusing on the negative things. That's the kind of faith I want to live with, a faith completely trusting God and knowing that nothing is too small in His eyes.

Life Lesson

When you face situations that seem impossible in your everyday life, God says, "I dare you to pray and ask Me for help." He wants to be good to you. He wants to show you His favor in new ways! Your heavenly Father wants the best for you, and nothing is too small in His eyes!

Chapter 15

Freedom Is Yours

For the weapons of our warfare *are* not carnal but mighty in God for pulling down strongholds, casting down arguments and every high thing that exalts itself against the knowledge of God, bringing every thought into captivity to the obedience of Christ, and being ready to punish all disobedience when your obedience is fulfilled.

2 Corinthians 10:4–6

If you heard John preach in person or on his weekly television program or have read his books, you realize that he was very transparent about the times in his life when he was confronted with depression and fear. There was one specific period of time when he went through an oppression and attack from the enemy, and through it all he learned, and I learned, to fight the good fight of faith.

In 1965, John had been pushing himself pretty hard in the ministry and perhaps wasn't taking as much time for himself as he should to be refreshed and strengthened. Then suddenly it just seemed that all the forces of hell came crashing down on him. One day as he drove down the highway, he said the oppression was so strong that he broke down and wept. That was not my John. He felt as though he was having a nervous collapse. Something very strange had happened to him, and it was alarming.

I wish I could say it ended that day, but this attack continued for a few months. John went from bad to worse. When I read that David said "innumerable evils have surrounded me . . . therefore my heart fails me" (Psalm 40:12), that might be an apt description of what came upon John. A hellish fear that he had never imagined could exist would grip him regarding every area of his life. The devil told him that he had a fatal illness, and then that he was dying of an unknown incurable disease. Maybe it was a brain tumor.

Sleep left him and insomnia tormented him. When morning came, he wished for night. When night came, he longed for morning. At times he said that his heart would pound so hard that he felt as though it was coming out of his chest. All initiative and the powerful drive he was known for left him. Everything about life was too overwhelming to think about. A little task would cause John to weep, because it seemed totally and absolutely impossible to do!

Looking back, it seemed like a never-ending nightmare. At the time, we didn't realize the devil was doing this to him. John had been trained in the Word of God in seminary and had preached for nineteen years, but neither of us knew much about our spiritual armor. We knew in a general sense that all bad things were from the devil, but we did not realize the level of spiritual attack he was under. And we didn't understand the power of the Word of God or how to use it. So while all of this oppression was on him, John was trying to minister to others the best he could.

"YOU'LL BE ALL RIGHT"

In the next chapter, I want to address more specifically the issue of fear that John experienced, but during the many months that this went on, we both sought the Lord with all our hearts for deliverance.

Other than me, John had not told anyone about his situation. He really couldn't even find the words to explain what he was going through to me. It was a spiritual battle that we didn't comprehend.

But then, thank God, He sent a man all the way from Fort Worth to Houston to encourage my husband. This man came to John and told him, "God sent me by here." He said that he had been through a similar experience, and God had brought him out of it. He said, "Pastor Osteen, you'll be all right. I've been where you are now. God brought me out, and He will bring you out too."

John told me that was the sweetest sentence he could ever hear! And the smile on his face was evidence. He had started to believe that he would never be all right again, but God wanted him to know that He would bring him through.

Hope was in his heart, and in my heart when I heard the good news, but John was not out of it yet. If he was going to help other believers rise up against the pressures of the forces of darkness, the only way he could was to come out of it by the Word of God.

In the midst of this battle, God reminded John of a dream He had given him many months before, but he hadn't connected it with what was going on. In that dream, John found himself in a small room, enclosed in the presence of Satan, the source of all fear and torment. In that vision, one poor man struggled impossibly to escape the room, but he could not open the door. This man finally crumpled to the floor, giving up in defeat. But John saw himself rise up as a strong soldier and said, "In the name of Jesus I will march out of this room!" He stood up and opened the door and marched out. When he remembered this dream, God spoke to him and said, "Do what you saw in the dream. Use the authority I have given you over Satan and you will be free!"

Thank God, John acted on what He told him to do that day. He arose from his knees and set his face like flint toward victory. He resisted the devil in the name of Jesus and declared

God's Word instead. He did not *feel* victory, but as he began to obey God, he got better and better.

John began to come out of that dark place. It was as though he'd been swimming underwater for weeks and finally was able to get his head above the surface and breathe again. It may appear that there is no easy way out of a situation like this, but there is! Jesus said, "I am the door" (John 10:7), and John walked through it.

What did John do? He turned to the Word of God and began to get the revelation he needed from the Bible. During those weeks and months of meditating upon the Word of God, he began to learn what Christ Jesus had purchased for him. He began to understand who he was in Christ. He began to comprehend his position of power and authority over the enemy. Faith began to rise up within him because of this revelation. It is the truth of God's Word that sets us free! He acted upon this truth and drove the enemy away.

It is the truth of God's Word that sets us free!

DECLARE THE WORD OF GOD

As John shared with me what he was learning, I realized that it was just as true for me as it was for him. Satan will try every way possible to defeat you, and unless you learn how to conquer him, you could go through an entire lifetime dominated by depression or fear or something else. I also began to fill my spirit and mind full of the Word of God. I began to confess who I was in Christ. I began to say daily what God said about me as a new creature.

We need to get rid of the idea that faith is a strange or mystical thing. Agree with what the Bible says: God has given you the measure of faith (Romans 12:3). Accept it as fact, and go on to grow in the principles of God.

Did this mean that we never had problems again? No, but it did mean we had weapons to fight and win the battle. After that ordeal, there were many times when John and I would remind each other to declare God's Word and resist the enemy in the name of Jesus.

You can do the same for yourself! As a believer, you have authority over Satan. James 4:7 says, "Resist the devil and he will flee from you." You must agree with what the Word says about you. What do I mean by that? Here are some basic scriptural examples for how you can agree with the Word of God:

• "I believe and agree with Romans 10:9–10, which states, 'If you confess with your mouth the Lord Jesus and believe in your heart that God has raised Him from the dead, you will be saved. For with the heart one believes unto righteousness, and with the mouth confession is made unto salvation.' Whether I feel saved or not, I agree with the Word of God. I confess Jesus as my Lord, and God says that I am saved. Therefore, I agree with His Word: I am saved. I have peace with God."

- Agree with God that you are a new creature in Christ Jesus. "I agree with 2 Corinthians 5:17: 'Therefore, if anyone *is* in Christ, *he is* a new creation; old things have passed away; behold, all things have become new.' I am a new creature in Christ. My past is forgiven, and I am a child of God. I agree with His Word. I thank God I am a new creature."

- In regards to physical, emotional, or mental healing, you can agree with 1 Peter 2:24 that "by [Jesus'] stripes you are healed." "I agree with God. By Jesus' stripes I am healed." When you hear a voice saying, "You will never be well," point to the Bible and say, "No, I agree with God. He cannot lie. His Word says, 'By whose stripes you were healed.' And I simply agree with God."

- When you've sinned, say, "Father, I am guilty. Your Word says, 'If I confess my sins, You are faithful and just to forgive my sins, and to cleanse me from all unrighteousness' (1 John 1:8–9). I agree with that scripture. I have confessed my sins, and You have kept Your end of the bargain. Therefore, no matter what I have done, I am cleansed by the blood of Jesus from all unrighteousness. I will not be under a cloud of condemnation about it. I agree with what Your Word says, and I am cleansed!"

- I believe that Jesus has given me authority to use His name. Luke 10:19 says, "I give you the authority to trample on serpents and scorpions, and over all the power of the enemy, and nothing shall by any means hurt you." Philippians 2:10 says, "that at the name of Jesus every knee should bow, of those in heaven, and of those on earth, and of those under the earth." I have power over Satan in the name of Jesus!

All too often we complicate the basics and lose the power of the Word of God. Some time ago, my little granddaughter Christiana was playing in my office. I had some little porcelain teacups there, and she knew she wasn't supposed to play with them. But when her mother turned her back, she did what little girls do and picked one up and pretended to drink out of it.

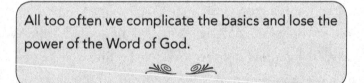

All too often we complicate the basics and lose the power of the Word of God.

However, when she went to put it back, the cup rattled against the saucer and made a lot of noise. She looked up at her mother, April, and burst out, "I'm sorry, Mommy!" Her expression told you how deeply she meant those words.

At that moment I thought, *That's the right way to handle it!* If we'd be just like a little child and confess our sins immediately, we would have God's mercy and forgiveness that quickly. Why? Because God can't resist our pleas for mercy when we're quick to confess!

Life Lesson

It may appear that there is no easy way out of a tough situation in your life, but Jesus said, "I am the door." Turn to the Word of God and begin to get the revelation you need. Meditate upon the Word and begin to understand who you are in Christ and your position of power and authority over Satan. Faith will rise up within you. It is the truth of God's Word that sets us free!

Chapter 16

Flying over Fear

Though a mighty army surrounds me,
my heart will not be afraid. Even if I am
attacked, I will remain confident.

Psalm 27:3 NLT

In the previous chapter, I said that I wanted to more specifically address the issue of fear because of what John went through during his bout with oppression in 1965. While the fear was a big portion of the anguish, he confronted and overcame his fear before he totally broke free from the oppression. In some ways, on top of all the other issues he was trying to deal with, the fear came as a double whammy.

John had been planning a speaking trip when a man came to him and prophesied that he had seen a vision of John getting on an airplane; then he saw the plane rise up in the air, burst into flames, and come down with a fiery crash. At the time we understood very little about a true prophetic word, and John took it seriously. A few years later, John would have realized that any prophecy should first be compared to the Word of God, and that prophecy is to edify, exhort, and comfort, not to cause fear. But it was all so new to us at the time. We know now that God never puts fear on us, because He has not given us a spirit of fear, but of power, love, and a sound mind (2 Timothy 1:6).

Although John had planned to fly on this trip, after hearing this warning he changed his mind and said he was taking the train instead. As we looked back on what happened as a result, we realized that the first mistake that he made was to act on fear. When you act on fear, things get worse. Fear activates Satan's power. Faith activates God's power.

Fear is a vapor, and fear is a lie, but if you let it in, it takes control of you. When John took that train, it was as though the fear of flying swallowed him up and engulfed him. It was so bad that the very thought of flying made him have cold sweats. The idea of flying on another trip was well past unthinkable.

> Fear is a vapor, and fear is a lie, but if you let it in, it takes control of you.

However, after a pastor from Fort Worth visited John and brought him the good news that God was going to bring him through this difficult time, John began to meditate upon the Word and understand his position and power in Christ over the enemy. Still, it didn't happen overnight.

But the day came when John returned to the place where he had acted on the fear of flying. He knew that he had to demonstrate Satan's defeat in this area where he had let the enemy dominate him. I was thrilled when he decided to confront his fear and take his next trip by airplane, but it was so hard on him! Fear has torment. Of course, the devil told him that the plane would fall out of the sky and he would never see our children and me again.

This time around, though, John had faith rising up to help him. He was determined now to act on his faith just as he had previously acted on his fear. He recognized that acting on fear had activated Satan, but that if he would act on faith, it would activate God.

Did he feel like flying? One glance at the lines on his forehead would tell you no. Would he have preferred the train? Absolutely. But John was adamant that it didn't matter how he felt. All that mattered was that he act like God told him the truth.

JUST WHEN YOU THINK YOU'RE READY

When John went to the airport that day, he thought he would have a four-engine jet, such as the Boeing 707, that would without doubt safely get him to his destination in spite of the fact that he was feeling so filled with anxiety. When he saw that it was a two-engine propeller plane, his knees got weak and he said that he almost fainted. He managed to get on the plane, sat down, and immediately broke out in a cold sweat.

But I know that Jesus smiled and the angels rejoiced, because they saw his determination to act on God's Word against Satan's lying fear. Jesus had deliberately left him in the arena of battle until he would take the sword of the Spirit and drive Satan away himself, albeit with drops of sweat! John quoted the promises of God all the way to his destination. When the devil reminded him of some of the recent airline crashes, John reminded him of what God had promised. He was bringing a demonstration that the devil was defeated in this area of his life!

I am well aware that John felt fear all the way to his destination, but the plane landed safely despite his feelings! That was a mighty big victory!

Nevertheless, the battle wasn't over. Then the devil told him, "John, you'll never get back home unless you walk." Well, that would have been a long walk, and the devil is a liar.

When he got back on the plane to come home, once again John did not feel God's presence. He did feel the grip of fear. But he acted like God told him the truth. God had said, "I will never leave you nor forsake you" (Hebrews 13:5). God had said in His Word, "No evil shall befall you . . . for He shall give His angels charge over you, to keep you in all your ways"

(Psalm 91:10–11). So John acted on those promises instead of the devil's lies!

Not only did his plane land safely, but thank God, Satan's power over John was broken and from that time on he flew all over the world so many times I lost count. It was funny because afterward, when he got on an airplane, he'd sit back in his seat and go to sleep. And he'd sleep so soundly that he'd wake up at his destination refreshed and ready to go, for all fear had been driven away! If John hadn't acted against fear, he would have never fulfilled his destiny, preaching the Gospel all over the world.

MY HEART SHALL KNOW NO FEAR

I am grateful that I never experienced the depths of fear that John battled and finally overcame through God's Word. But no one has ever lived who hasn't felt the grip of fear surrounding them at some point. I faced it in a major way when I was diagnosed with cancer. You may know that same battle with cancer or another illness and perhaps are fighting the fear right now. None of us are immune to the fears that arise regarding our lives, our spouse, our children, our income, and many other things.

Because people have seen me so often on the church platform over the years, they think I must have been a natural as John was. That's hardly the case. For many years John tried to get me up on that platform with him. Not only was I afraid to get up there, but pastors' wives just didn't do that at the time. John felt it would be a good thing for the church, and he kept encouraging me that I had the gifts and the ability to do it. He said it was part of my destiny. I wasn't so sure . . . not at all.

But after I was healed of cancer in 1981, so much changed as my faith increased. I learned how important a touch from God really is, and I realized that every time our congregation saw me, they saw a miracle to encourage their faith, because I was supposed to have been dead. I gradually started doing announcements and greetings, then I began to pray for the sick, and I realized that God had more for me. At a time when very few if any women participated with their husbands in ministry, I came into a place of actually feeling comfortable in front of the church. I don't preach, but I love to share out of my heart.

I know how it is when things come against us in life— sickness; issues with children, relatives, friends, work, public criticism; and things like that. Sometimes it just seems as though we're overwhelmed with fears.

I read the book of Psalms every month, and there's a little phrase, ". . . My heart shall not fear," that may help you. It has helped me countless times.

We can either refuse to allow fear in our heart or we can be fearful. But this scripture says we don't have to have fear. The Word of God says, ". . . My heart shall not fear," and I believe it. If you have the Word of God in your heart, it will be protected and you can live your life without fear.

NOT EVEN DEATH CAN HURT US

John liked to tell a story from his childhood about a big, old, spooky two-story house that he; his brother, Jack; and their friends thought was haunted. One late fall evening, Jack and John were sitting on a curb across the street from that foreboding empty house. Jack was about ten years old, and John was eight. Both were fearful, but in the evening shadows, John was growing more frightened by the minute.

Suddenly Jack just stood up and said, "I'm going in there."

It was almost dark and John remembered thinking, *I'll never see my big brother again!*

Some other boys joined John on the curb, and they held their breaths and waited together while Jack investigated the "haunted" house all by himself. Pretty soon Jack showed up on the upper-story balcony and shouted down, "It's all right, fellas. I've been through this old house, and there's nothing in here that can hurt us!"

That's how Jesus is when we're frightened about something. Isaiah 40:4 says He goes before us and makes crooked places straight. To me, this means He checks things out for us and lets us know if and when it's safe to proceed.

There are a lot of things that people fear, especially death and dying. But Jesus marched down into the jaws of hell itself and wrestled with the principalities and powers of darkness for three days and nights. And on the third day, He came out! His cry to you and me is, "There is nothing in death to hurt you if you'll make Me your Lord and Savior!"

There is nothing to fear from anything or anyone when Jesus is your Lord!

> There is nothing to fear from anything or anyone when Jesus is your Lord!

Life Lesson

When you act on fear, you are saying by your actions that the enemy is mightier than God. When you act on the Word of God in faith against fear, you are demonstrating that God is greater than the devil. Acting on the Word of God in faith activates the power of God!

Chapter 17
Miracles behind "The Miracle"

You intended to harm me, but God intended
it all for good. He brought me to this position so I could save the lives of many people.

Genesis 50:20 NLT

January 30, 1990, is a day that is forever etched deeply into
my life and the life of our family, and no one more so than my
daughter Lisa. In some ways it is still very much of a blur in my
mind, almost as though it didn't or couldn't have happened. It
was the unthinkable day when Lisa was in our church offices
and opened a brown package smaller than a shoe box that was
addressed personally to John. It exploded in her lap and blew
her across the room, about six feet from her desk.

The number of miracles that surrounded her surviving
the blast are too many to document in this chapter, but for

Lisa they started early that morning with her having second thoughts about the outfit she was going to wear that day. Initially, she was going to wear a cotton skirt and blouse, but she had an impulse to change into her black leather skirt and a jacket, and she did, although she really didn't understand why until after the explosion.

Lisa was working as our director of ministries at Lakewood at the time, and she routinely opened personal mail for both her father and me. We received a lot of mail from people requesting prayer or writing to encourage us, and people would send us occasional gifts of books and sermon tapes.

This box had come in the morning mail addressed to John and was heavy and rattled funny when Lisa shook it. Curious about its contents, she picked it up and put it down three times that morning, but other office matters interrupted. After some time, around 10:30 a.m., she picked it up again and gave it another shake; then she sat down at her desk, put the box in her lap sideways, and tugged on the tape on the top of the box.

In that moment the lights went out for Lisa . . . and in the room. When she awoke, she was somehow standing against the wall across the office in the darkness, her body shaking violently, her clothes smoldering, with the intense smell of chemicals burning her nostrils.

Because of the configuration of the offices, the other staff members heard the blast but weren't even sure if it came from within the offices. John's executive assistant, Renee, thought it sounded as though an eighteen-wheeler semi had slammed into the side of our office building. By the time any of the staff located the blast site, Lisa had somehow managed to stumble out of her office and was calling out, "A bomb! It's a bomb!"

Lois, our receptionist, made her way through the billowing smoke in the hallway and found Lisa with smoldering pieces of debris in her hair, and she and our accountant, Phyllis, pulled off Lisa's jacket and leather skirt that were covered with tiny embers and threatening to start to burn. If Lisa had worn her cotton outfit, she surely would have been burned badly. A miracle can come in the form of what outfit you wear on a given day.

Somehow in the chaos, 911 was called, and then we got the call at home, "Lisa is all right, but she's been in an explosion. She does have some injuries on her leg and abdomen." In that moment, time was suspended and the world may as well have stopped spinning. I heard the words, but the words made no sense. The shock wave of it rolled over me, and it was as though my heart and mind and nerves suddenly went numb. I could not comprehend it.

The building was evacuated and simultaneously the firefighters and police and emergency medical teams poured in. As the chaotic scene unfolded, an ambulance arrived in about ten minutes, and the paramedics lifted Lisa onto a gurney and then into the ambulance. Amazingly, one of the paramedics leaned in and said, "Lisa, as soon as we close the door, I am going to pray for you." And he did, which brought Lisa a deep peace and calmness as the ambulance headed to Hermann Hospital. God knew exactly what Lisa needed in that moment, even the right paramedic, and He was right there with her.

When Lisa was wheeled into the emergency room and being prepared to transfer to Methodist Hospital for treatment, the paramedic who had prayed for her gasped when he saw her wounds. They were not nearly as terrible looking as they had been when he first saw them in the church office. During that twenty-minute ride to the hospital, God had already begun to heal the tears and burns.

Even before Lisa arrived at the second hospital, reporters from the *Houston Chronicle*, radio newscasters, and even CNN had gathered there. The story headline went nationwide and around the world: BOMB HURTS PASTOR'S DAUGHTER. LAKEWOOD CHURCH TARGET OF EXPLOSION.

You cannot imagine the number of calls, letters, and flowers that poured in to Lisa's room from around the world. The city of Houston and local churches and churches from every denomination reached out in such a loving way. When tragedy strikes and the chips are down, John said later, the people of God of all backgrounds love one another. President George H. W. Bush, in office at the time, even called, offering his condolences, expressing concern, and assuring us that investigators would do everything possible to find who committed the crime at Lakewood. We so appreciated his call and concern.

Meanwhile, a series of doctors began to explore the intensity of Lisa's wounds. She needed surgery to repair three holes in her abdomen and a larger hole in her right leg that destroyed a portion of muscle tissue and needed to be closed, but no skin grafts were required. She was expected to be in the hospital for weeks, but thirteen days later she had recovered. The rapidness of her healing from such serious injuries surprised even the doctors. Lisa will always have reminders: a ten-inch scar, resembling a shepherd's staff, across her stomach and a five-inch scar and slight indentation on her right leg.

As officials from the Alcohol, Tobacco, and Firearms division and FBI moved in and questioned every member of our family as well as people at our church, the seriousness of the crime began to sink in. That bomb was meant to kill my beloved John, and it nearly took my beloved Lisa. And whoever sent it was still out there. Even though Lisa's story was later broadcast through the popular television show *Unsolved Mysteries*, which generated more than five hundred calls and leads after the first airing, the crime has never been solved.

Investigators said it was a miracle Lisa survived at all, let alone with just two scars. Bomb experts determined that the mail bomb actually malfunctioned. Instead of exploding all over Lisa's body as intended, it blew out both ends, and because Lisa turned the box sideways in her lap, it directed the blast away from her. That rattle she heard when she shook the package was the rubbing of shrapnel against ten-inch nails—metals that upon explosion blasted a significant hole in her desk, and pocked the walls with gashes, slashes, and holes. It was a miracle Lisa wasn't injured more!

"It was as if someone was standing between Lisa and the bomb," one of the paramedics at the scene was quoted as saying.

We knew exactly who that someone was, and I am still praising Him today.

MORE MIRACLES BEFORE "THE MIRACLE"

What most people don't know about January 30, 1990, is what went on in our home that morning to keep John from being in the office to open that package himself. It is amazing how God goes before us to protect us from harm and even comfort us before a disaster arrives.

Early on the morning when the devil tried to take John's life, and nearly took Lisa's life, and tried to destroy the church, John had a supernatural experience in our home. He said it was as though the Lord shook him and woke him up long before daylight. He went to the den, got his Bible, and when he sat down, the presence of Jesus came into the room and overwhelmed my husband. He began to weep and worship Him, and as he did, God began to open up several scriptures to him, who had no idea that someone was intent on taking his life that day.

The scriptures that Jesus gave John that day were not just

for John, but for Lisa, for our family, for our church, and for you as you read them now:

"Preserve me, O God, for in You I put my trust . . . I have set the LORD always before me; because *He is* at my right hand I shall not be moved. Therefore my heart is glad, and my glory rejoices; my flesh also will rest in hope" (Psalm 16:1, 8–9). Jesus is real; He's alive, and He is here to preserve us.

"You have tested my heart; You have visited *me* in the night; You have tried me and have found nothing; I have purposed that my mouth shall not transgress. Concerning the works of men, by the word of Your lips, I have kept away from the paths of the destroyer" (Psalm 17:3–4). Someone was out to destroy my husband, but the Lord was not going to allow it!

"For You have armed me with strength for the battle; You have subdued under me those who rose up against me" (Psalm 18:39).

"May the LORD answer you in the day of trouble; may the name of the God of Jacob defend you" (Psalm 20:1).

On and on the Lord spoke to John in a supernatural way, and while he didn't understand exactly what the Lord was meaning, he received it into his spirit. And in the midst of that visitation in the night's lingering darkness, John lifted up every member of our family. He did not know what we were going to face, but when it came, we were prepared and ready.

Then he looked down at his Bible and read, " 'It shall come to pass that before they call, I will answer; and while they are still speaking, I will hear' " (Isaiah 65:24). Hallelujah! That is exactly what God did.

> "It shall come to pass that before they call, I will answer; and while they are still speaking, I will hear."
>
> ~⊚ ⊚~

The second miracle was that God supernaturally kept John at our house that morning. Normally, if he got up way before daylight, which he did often, he would read his Bible and pray, enjoy his cup of coffee, and be at the church office when it opened. But every time he tried to leave the house, something interrupted him. He kept saying, "I *have* to get down to the church *now*," but it was as though an angel was pushing him back. John said, "I don't know what's wrong, but I can't get out of the house." And finally he literally just gave up. That was not like John in the least bit. It would take angels to keep him away from church.

So when the call came around 10:45 a.m., John was still at home, alive and safe. People asked, "Why do you think God kept him home and had Lisa there?" We don't know, but God knew the situation completely and had everyone in His care. Would that bomb have killed John? I don't know. Only God can explain it, but we know what He did! I can't tell you why it happened, but it did happen this way.

We also marveled that God kept every other one of our church staff out of Lisa's office. Any number of people could have been in there, and if they had been, they would have been in the blast zone of the nails and shrapnel. God is interested and is involved in the affairs of our lives—yes, every footstep we take and every encounter we make, and when and where. As believers, we have God's supernatural protection.

When Lisa returned to church, she preached a powerful message about how we can walk through the fires and trials of life and come out unaffected, and that is exactly what she did. Even when you walk "through the valley of the shadow of death," as Lisa did, God will walk with you and guide your steps out of the valley. Keep following Him, and He will bring you to the mountaintop and prepare a table for you in the very presence of your enemies.

Life Lesson

Remember that God always stands between us and the enemy of our souls. He may come against us to steal, kill, and destroy, but before we call out to God, He will answer; and while we are still speaking, He will hear. God is interested and is involved in the affairs of our lives—yes, every footstep we take and every encounter we make, and when and where.

Chapter 18

Lessons from a Man's Best Friend

David was greatly distressed because the people spoke of stoning him, for all of them were embittered, each man for his sons and daughters. But David felt strengthened *and* encouraged in the LORD his God.

1 Samuel 30:6 AMP

When our children were growing up, we had a wonderful family dog named Scooter that came about thigh high on an adult. He was a great big German shepherd, and he was loved by everyone . . . most of the time . . . and most of all by our children. Scooter was so playful and just plain fun to be around, and he provided us more than one dog's lifetime of memories. Every child should have at least one Scooter to enjoy while they are growing up.

Scooter would let the children tug on his tail and wrestle with him on the lawn. He loved to play fetch with the boys, and I don't remember how many times I looked out the window to see Scooter dashing in and out of the sprinkler on the front lawn. He was strong and fast, always chasing squirrels here and there, always on the go.

His escapades were not limited to the daytime hours, however. Scooter had a strong nocturnal bent to him and would prowl the neighborhood after the sun was long set and the stars were out, gathering various and sundry unwanted items from who knows where for our family inspection in the morning. Standing proudly in the sparkling dew grass of a new day, there would be Scooter with his piles of discoveries from the night adventures, contentedly wagging his tail and waiting for our approval. It might be a single glove or a lady's right shoe or some other souvenirs. One morning we woke to discover that he'd dragged home a red-and-blue Big Wheel Racer.

As I said, they loved Scooter most of the time. There were those moments, though, such as the night when he got into the neighbor's rabbit pen. If you can imagine how we reacted when we opened the front door that following morning to a smiling Scooter and his collection of dead rabbits! Not our best day in the neighborhood.

At one point Scooter had caused enough mischief in the

neighborhood that we felt he had to go, despite the agony and tears that it caused the children. We had friends who lived about seven miles away and were willing to give Scooter a new home, which also meant that the children could see him occasionally. That didn't last long, though. One day we had a big thunderstorm, and in the mysterious ways of the dog world, Scooter, who was terribly frightened by thunderstorms, somehow found his way home. We couldn't believe it when we walked into the garage after the storm, and there was good old Scooter, curled up in the corner where he always went when he was afraid. He came back to his safe place in our home that he knew so well.

BE BIG ON THE INSIDE

John was so proud of that dog, the king of the neighborhood, and he bragged on Scooter everywhere he went. John said that Scooter was so big and strong and healthy looking that he could "whip" a lion and run like a deer. It was John's ritual to take Scooter along with him on his bike rides, winding in and out of the subdivisions near our house. Scooter would prance alongside John like a thoroughbred, holding his head up high with his muscles rippling. He seemed to be fearless, as if he would defeat anything that got in his way and protect John against any foe. The two of them were a sight.

One bright sunny day my husband was riding along with

his fine dog trotting by his side. Suddenly a spunky little Chihuahua about the size of a rabbit came charging out of a passing yard toward Scooter. Its legs were hardly bigger than matchsticks. As John watched him bark, he thought, *Watch out, little dog! You are messing with the wrong dog. Scooter can put one paw on you and you'd be a goner! He'll eat you up with one bite.*

But that tiny dog kept coming with full force, yapping and barking up a storm. John thought about restraining Scooter by the collar. He was concerned that Scooter would tear that dog up. But before he could get his bike stopped, the little dog arrived full speed, growling, tail tucked, teeth bared.

Then much to John's utter dismay and surprise, Scooter hung his head in a cowardly fashion, rolled over on his back, put up all four feet, and gave up! Whatever that little dog said in dog talk, maybe giving Scooter orders never to come that way again, he was convincing!

My husband was devastated to think that a little tiny dog had overpowered his mighty dog. He came home shaking his head in disgust. Apparently Scooter was not nearly as big on the inside as he was on the outside.

WHEN ADVERSITY COMES BARKING

We've all done something similar, right? Adversity comes barking and baring its teeth, declaring, "You're not going to get well. You have all the symptoms again. You are going to be penniless. You are going to lose this and lose that. You will never be free of your addiction." And too often we act just like Scooter and back down, roll over, tremble in fear, and throw in the towel.

When we surrender like that, it makes no more sense than Scooter cowering before a Chihuahua. We have the most powerful force in the universe inside us. We are made to be more than conquerors. God destined us to live in victory. But for whatever reason, we just give up and say, "I can't do this. It's too tough for me."

If you get knocked down, don't stay down. It's time to stand up on the inside! When David came into a period of extreme distress, rather than give up he encouraged and strengthened himself in the Lord our God. Use the name of Jesus and tap into God's power! Stand strong and fight the good fight of faith. Don't yield to the enemy one thing God has given you. It does not belong to him. You have a legal document. It is written in the Word of God. This legal document says abundant life is yours.

Stand strong and fight the good fight of faith.

No matter what comes against you in life, make a firm decision to keep standing up on the inside!

Life Lesson

We have the most powerful force in the universe inside us. We are made to be more than conquerors. God destined us to live in victory. If you get knocked down, don't stay down. Encourage and strengthen yourself in the Lord our God. No matter what comes against you in life, make a firm decision to keep standing up on the inside!

Chapter 19

44 Years, 4 Months, and 6 Days

So whether we are here in this body or away from this body, our goal is to please him.

2 Corinthians 5:9 NLT

I was married to my best friend for forty-four years, four months, and six days, and I am grateful for *every* second of it. None of us ever expected John to leave us so soon, and we surely weren't prepared for it. But Jesus always has a way of helping us through storms in our lives. He is always there to guide us. If we never had trials, we would never know of His great mercy and grace to bring us through!

> Jesus always has a way of helping us through storms in our lives. He is always there to guide us.
>
> ◦◦ ◦◦

My husband fought hypertension since he was in his forties, but it never kept him from preaching the good news of Jesus all over the world. He preached even when he didn't feel like it!

One time we were in a conference, and in the middle of the night John woke up feeling extremely dizzy. The next morning he asked two men to escort him up onto the platform just in case, and he sat on a stool to preach.

On a morning in 1987, John was scheduled for a CT angiogram. He got up early, went into the den, grabbed a globe we kept in there, held it to his chest, and prayed over it. He prayed, "God, I have so much more to do for You." He was always thinking of the nations and the unreached masses. That very morning they performed an emergency bypass surgery.

Still, he traveled overseas many times after that surgery, conquering anything that faced him. In fact, one of the last things he did was travel to India. He washed the feet of some of his missionary friends and invested money into those he knew could effectively evangelize the world. He was that kind of man. When God gave him an assignment, he always did it and did it well. I admired him tremendously.

Over the years, God spared John's life several times, but from that first bypass surgery on, his condition slowly worsened, his blood pressure remained elevated, and eventually his kidneys stopped functioning normally, so he began dialysis in 1998, three months before his death.

I know people could tell that my husband was sick because he looked it. You could see the fatigue in his eyes. But when I told him that we needed to tell the church about his starting dialysis, he was hesitant because he was a little embarrassed. It took a little bit of convincing, but he finally agreed. So one afternoon we called a staff meeting in our conference room in our former Lakewood administration building.

When the time came for my husband to speak to the people, he didn't want to go. Instead he asked me to deliver the news to them. I didn't want to either, but I wanted to help my husband feel at ease. So I went out and told the people about his condition and about his plans to begin dialysis treatment. The people's response was unexpected but absolutely beautiful. After a moment of suspended silence, a loud eruption of applause broke out. Finally, I was able to persuade him to come out and sit on a stool. Some of us got down and rubbed his swollen feet. It was such a touching moment that I will cherish it in my heart forever.

You know, that is the picture I believe God has in His heart for His church. He wants it to be a family—a group of people who will stand by you through your darkest times as well as your best times. He wants it to be a people who will "rub your feet," so to speak, when you get tired and feel that you can't go on, so that you can stand up again and jump back into the race that God has for you. That's who the people of Lakewood were for us, and I am eternally grateful for them! And they are still like that!

> God wants His church to be a family—a group of people who will stand by you through your darkest times as well as your best times.

A MEDICAL MINISTRY

John started on dialysis in the fall of 1998. He was seventy-seven at that time. A few times a week, I would take him to the dialysis center. It was normal for the course to find him ministering to the other patients there, before and after his treatment. With my husband, every moment had a purpose. I never saw him waste an opportunity to reach out to someone else in need, even if he was the one hurting the most.

I still remember the look on his face when Joel asked him if he would like a dialysis machine brought into our house to eliminate his trips to the hospital. John looked at him sternly and said, "No, Joel. I have to see my friends at the dialysis center." John loved doing special things for his friends there. The Christmas before he went to Heaven, he had the church have a Christmas dinner for them. He loved finding practical ways to share the love of Jesus.

That just shows you what kind of man he really was—a man who always strived to put others' needs above his own, even in the midst of his own pain. Up until his last days on earth, he truly lived out these words from the apostle Paul: "Let each of you look not only to his own interests, but also to the interests of others" (Philippians 2:4 ESV). He did this in the church as well, remaining in the pulpit every week up until a month before he went to Heaven.

Today, when I am faced with an opportunity to be selfish, I often stop and ask myself, "What would my husband do?" or "How would he respond?" I never want to spend my life focused only on my own well-being, because a life lived only for ourselves is really no life at all! Jesus lived to serve, and we are to be imitators of Him. That is becoming increasingly difficult to do, as we live in a culture that is extremely obsessed with self. But it is vital to the kingdom of God that we take His command seriously. God has called each of us to be a light in the darkness, to spread His hope to each and every person with whom we come in contact. How can we do that when we are only focused on ourselves?

> God has called each of us to be a light in the darkness.

SAYING GOOD-BYE

John went to Heaven on Saturday, January 23, 1999. Looking back, the days leading up to our final good-bye were filled with several special moments that I will cherish forever. The Wednesday before John went to Heaven, we both stumbled into the house after a hospital visit, completely worn out. When dinnertime came around, John said, "Sweetheart, I sure would like to have a steak."

Oh my! I was so tired. I knew how much John loved steak, and I wanted to please him. So I went to the Taste of Texas restaurant to get him one. They wouldn't even let me pay for it. Little did I know that would be his last steak and one of my last chances to serve him a meal.

The Friday before John's death, Oral Roberts came to visit. We had a wonderful time together, and he prayed over him. At the time we had no idea that would be John's final good-bye to his longtime friend. It was later that night, after Oral had left and we had just lain down in bed, that John started having trouble breathing. He asked me to go upstairs and get him another pillow, so I did. I placed it under his head and then lay at the foot of the bed. I looked at him for a moment; then out of nowhere I asked, "Sweetheart, you're not going to leave me, are you?"

He looked back and said confidently, "Never." If only we had known!

John could see that I was exhausted, so after a few minutes, he told me that he was going to go sit in his recliner in the den for a while because he didn't want to keep me up. I responded with a sleepy "Okay" and fell asleep. The next thing I knew, it was 2:30 a.m. and my son-in-law Gary was knocking on my bedroom door. The first words that came out of his mouth stunned me: *"Mama, Daddy quit breathing!"*

John had called Gary to come over and visit with him because he couldn't sleep. Gary says that they were having a conversation about all that John was going through and that conversation left him with John's last words on earth. He looked at Gary, smiled, and uttered: "Thank God, His mercy endures forever."

In that moment John's heart stopped. We called the paramedics, and they took him to the hospital. They placed him on life support in our den. We wanted to keep him on it for a few hours so that as much of our family as possible could cherish our final moments with him.

At one point I turned around and couldn't find April, who was very pregnant at the time. I asked where she was and someone told me that she went home and would be right back. In just a few minutes she returned and placed a picture of her most recent ultrasound on John's pillow. She was so sad that he wouldn't get to see her baby. Ten days after the funeral, she had our grandbaby Elliana Elise.

Not long after that, April had a dream about her daddy. He was sitting out on her porch swing by her big bay window in his favorite leather jacket. She was inside when her eyes met his through the window. He simply looked at her, smiled, and said, "You did good, April." Jesus knew just how to comfort her!

Of course, we also called Jim and Tamara, who live in Victoria, Texas, and Justin, John's oldest son, who was living in New York at the time. I was sitting in that cold hospital room, hearing the silence broken by little footsteps running down the hall. They kept getting louder until I saw little Tamara turning quickly around the corner. Out of breath, she whispered, "Did we make it?"

Thankfully, they did, and we were all able to say our final good-byes to John—the most incredible husband and father. Although he was on life support, I believe his spirit was still in the room during those last couple of hours. In our final moments together as a family, we took turns talking to him and singing songs to him. Lisa's husband, Kevin, suggested we wash John's feet, and it was a beautiful time together. I believe that John was with us that day as we lovingly sent him home. Sam Martin, his longtime friend, came to see John, too. Then the children and I went into the hallway and decided to release our loved one to go to be with Jesus.

After John was taken off life support, we all filed into the waiting room and just sat there, a bit stunned to be honest. Everything had happened so quickly that none of us could believe that he was actually gone. Just then, one of John's dear pastor friends, Dr. Bill Hinson, the pastor of First Methodist Church in Houston, walked into the room. He had heard that

John was in the hospital, so he came to find us. The hospital staff told him that they weren't allowed to give him the room number, so he walked around searching for us until he found us.

I felt that this man was God-sent that day as he sat with us and ministered to us, only minutes after John's passing. The peace of God flooded that hospital room, and in that moment I knew that everything was going to be all right. I was reminded that God never leaves His children. Yes, He always has a plan, and He alone has the power to turn a broken heart into something beautiful. He repairs broken hearts.

John always said that he would live and preach into his nineties. He said he would rather "shoot high and miss it than shoot low and make it." He died in faith, even with his last words declaring the mercy of the Lord that endures forever. He was still magnifying God and crossed the finish line with his fire still burning. He died believing for healing, and that's just what He got, just not on this side of Heaven.

Sometimes when things happen, they don't make sense to us. There are many times we feel like asking God, "Why? Why my loved one? Why now?" It's in those moments we must remember that it's not up to us to hold God accountable for His secrets, because the secret things belong to Him. He holds us accountable for the things He has revealed to us (Deuteronomy 29:29). After all, if God's ways were simple enough for us to understand, they probably wouldn't be worth pursuing!

THE HOMEGOING OF MY BELOVED

When word got out about John's death, the newspaper and television media were absolutely wonderful. His homegoing was everything I dreamed it could be. Thousands of people from all across the world came for his memorial service, to salute him and to honor what a great man of God he was. Many people shed tears without ever having known him personally.

The thing is, you didn't have to know my husband personally to feel as though you knew him. People everywhere viewed him as a mentor and as a father figure. That day I heard so many stories about how he had helped people whom I had never even met! He was such a kind and compassionate man, so full of faith.

We honored our hero by having a bagpiper play "Amazing Grace" as they carried John's casket around the church that he loved so much one last time. Though I had my hard moments during the service, I felt at peace because I knew John was more alive at that moment than he had ever been in this life. He had no more heart or kidney disease but was rejoicing on the streets of gold.

I kept envisioning the Indians whom John had loved so much, those who had gone on before him, lining up to hug him and to love on him. I pictured his daddy who had given his heart to Jesus in one of his meetings waiting to give him a great big hug. What an entrance John must have had! Thank

God that today he is in the grandstands cheering us on—and we won't let you down, sweetheart!

What do you think it will be like when we meet Jesus someday? Will we be ashamed to think of what we didn't do for Him, or will we be happy that we did exactly what He asked us to do? I hope to make an entrance like John made. My prayer is that we all get to Heaven and hear these cherished words from our Savior: "Well done, My good and faithful servant."

Life Lesson

Sometimes when things happen, they don't make sense to us. There are many times we feel like asking God, "Why? Why my loved one? Why now?" It's in those moments we must remember that it's not up to us to hold God accountable for His secrets, because the secret things belong to Him. After all, if God's ways were simple enough for us to understand, they probably wouldn't be worth pursuing!

Chapter 20

Filling John's Shoes

❧

"For I know the plans I have for you," says the LORD. "They are plans for good and not for disaster, to give you a future and a hope."

Jeremiah 29:11 NLT

As with many other people's homegoings, John didn't plan on going to Heaven when he did. So he hadn't appointed any one person to take over as the pastor of Lakewood Church. He had told Lisa a couple of times that if anything ever happened to him, the Holy Spirit would show us what to do. Well, he was right. Jesus helped us to know exactly what to do, but it took a while; although not as long as I thought it would.

Today, after having Joel as pastor for seventeen years, it's hard to remember that he had never preached a message in his life until the last Sunday before John's death. Over the course of Joel's seventeen years at Lakewood as the manager of our television production, John had tried many times to get Joel out in public to preach, but he didn't even *want* to make announcements! He had always been content to work behind the scenes, and he did it so well.

But about a week before John went to be with the Lord, we were at Kevin and Lisa's home for dinner. During the meal, John said to us, "I'm going to ask Joel if he'll speak for me this Sunday."

I laughed and said, "John, you're just wasting your time. Joel is not going to get out there and speak in front of everybody."

That didn't keep John from calling right from the table, and Joel responded as he had so many times, "Daddy, I'm not a preacher. You're the preacher. You get up there and preach, and I promise you this: I'll make you look good."

What we didn't know was that Joel couldn't dismiss his daddy's words this time, and for the first time in his life, he suddenly had an overwhelming desire to preach. Although he had never even prepared a sermon previously or preached before thousands of people and millions via the television broadcast, he called my husband back and said, "Daddy, I've changed my mind. I'll do it."

We were stunned!

So Joel went to work on a sermon and delivered his first sermon the following Sunday, which was well received by the congregation. Lisa and Victoria and Joel went to see John after that service and said that he looked so proud. He had listened to Joel from his hospital room and was telling the nurses all about it. When he asked Lisa how she thought Joel did, her reply was, "I think someday he might be standing in front of the camera instead of behind it."

John passed away five days later, and we had church that Sunday and grieved the loss of my husband as a bereaved congregation. Our dear friend Pastor Sam Carr spoke for us that day and brought great comfort to us. We were planning a special memorial service in John's honor for the following Wednesday, and in the midst of that week, Joel called me and said, "Mother, who is speaking this Sunday?"

I replied, "Well, I don't know, Joel. We are going to pray and believe that God will send the right one."

There was a pause, then Joel said, "Well, I'm sort of thinking about . . . maybe that I would like to do it."

Joel may have been still debating it in his mind, but that was good enough for me. I hung up before he had a chance to say another word. Two days later, at John's memorial service with eight thousand people in attendance, I turned around and looked at Joel and said, "I'm so happy to announce to you that my son Joel will be preaching this Sunday."

"WE ARE NOT GOING BACKWARD!"

Joel did great that Sunday, but I wasn't exactly sure what to do about the future. Joel had never preached but twice! He says that he shook a lot and couldn't understand why everyone was staring at him! All the children helped preach during this time, and we had guest speakers occasionally to help with our three weekly services.

But at the start, it was obvious that everyone loved Joel and looked to him as the pastor. Every time he walked onto the platform, the congregation applauded. Even when he messed up, they cheered for him, and they still do! When he got emotional, you could hear people yelling out, "We love you, Joel!" They'd clap and clap until he regained his composure. It sort of reminded me of the story of David, when everyone cheered for David before he was even the king. It's as though they knew God had anointed Joel as pastor before he was the pastor! I'm sure John was jumping up and down in Heaven.

Not long after that, Joel called me and said, "I think God has led me to pastor the church."

I thought, *Oh, dear, are you sure?* because, though I loved to hear him speak, the mother inside of me was not sure if he could handle the pressure of the leadership as his daddy had. But I prayed about it and felt that Joel was right. We were sure that he was to be the next pastor of Lakewood Church.

For many years Victoria had encouraged Joel that one day he would be preaching. She would tell him, "Joel, you've got so much to offer. God is going to use you. You've got what it takes. Just preach to the people the way you preach to me!" That may have made Joel nervous, but her confidence and belief in him planted seeds inside him and helped enlarge his vision for what God was calling him to do.

Immediately after John went to heaven, one of the first things Joel did was to cancel our national television broadcast that aired Sunday night on the Family Channel. Joel thought that if he was preaching, no one would want to listen. But when Victoria heard what he'd done, she told him to call the company sales representative back and keep that time. "We're not going to go backward, Joel!" she told him. "We're not going to shrink back in fear. There are people all over the world who are watching to see what happens to Lakewood. We need that TV time!"

Fortunately, before Joel was even able to make contact with the sales representative, who had immediately found a new buyer for that valuable time slot, the representative felt something inside say, "Don't change the contract until next week." God providentially kept us on the Family Channel, which became a major step in our future growth.

Even though we knew within a couple of months of John's passing that Joel was to be the next pastor of Lakewood, we decided to wait until October to announce our decision to the church. We wanted to be sure that we were hearing from God and not just making a decision on our own, and it gave Joel time to adjust to his new role.

Never in a hundred years did I expect Joel to pastor Lakewood because he liked being behind the scenes, but thank God, He had other plans! Joel is living out his calling. He has stepped up to the plate and has truly surprised us all.

I was so touched the day his brother, Paul, told me, "Mother, Joel used to be my little brother, but now he's my pastor." I am extremely proud of my children and their spouses, not because they are successful, but because they are doing exactly what Jesus has asked them to do. Thank God, He always has a plan for us and He never leaves us. Ever!

STEPPING IN

Joel became the official pastor of Lakewood Church in October 1999, and he has been tremendous. For the first year he preached wearing his daddy's shoes, literally, which was precious to me. He was so close to John. In fact, he says his dad was his best friend, and he really did learn so much from working with him.

It has been wonderful watching how Joel has progressed. He was so nervous at first. I remember leaning over to him every service before he would go up on the platform and telling him, "Joel, you are remarkable." I wanted him to know that we believed in him.

As time has gone on, he has proven that he is confident in his own shoes. He preaches messages that touch millions of people's lives every week. I am constantly amazed at his discipline. He studies hard and takes the office to which God has assigned him very seriously. His time is really not his own now, because he wants to please the one who called him. I salute him.

At first our goal was just to maintain the church. I remember an article that was published in the *Houston Chronicle* by several professors and theologians shortly after John's death. They predicted in the article that a megachurch that lost its leader would go down. They said that the worst thing that could happen is that one of the sons takes over, especially because John was such a strong leader. Thank God, His plan is always greater. When He wants something done, no one can stop it!

Since Joel took over, God not only helped us maintain the church, but it has grown by leaps and bounds. Today we meet in the former Compaq Center and have nearly forty-five thousand people in our services every week. What a miracle! Only God could have caused things to happen as they have. He knows each person's calling and abilities, and if we follow His voice, He will use us in great ways.

> God knows each person's calling and abilities, and if we follow His voice, He will use us in great ways.

If we want God to use us, though, we must realize that His ways are not our ways. His thoughts are higher than ours. If we limit God, we will limit ourselves. We may be able to do *some* things on our own, but if we want to reach our *full* potential, we must rely on God's help. *He chooses ordinary people to do extraordinary things!* But we must be willing, even when we don't feel we're quite ready for the challenge.

What is God asking you to do? Do you feel inadequate? Always remember that you can stand in your heavenly Father's shoes. He promises to see you through, no matter how hard the task. If He has called you, He will equip you!

PAUL'S CALL

It thrills my heart to see my children carry out their daddy's dreams, not because they feel obligated, but because they have the same heart.

When Paul was twelve years old, he went to South Africa with his dad. Paul tells how while he was there, Jesus spoke to his heart that he would someday return as a medical doctor.

Sure enough, Paul went to medical school and became an excellent general surgeon in the great hospital of Little Rock, Arkansas. I was thrilled because I love medicine so much. He had so much success on top of his busy surgical practice over the years—a beautiful plot of land, a gorgeous home, a nice income, everything for which he had worked so hard. However, on the way home from John's memorial service, God spoke to Paul's heart to give up his practice and return to Houston to help with the church. Jennifer, his wife, was in full agreement.

Paul was thrilled, and the more he considered it, the more the peace of God flooded his heart. God sometimes asks us to do things we haven't thought of or things we wouldn't naturally want to do, but if we are obedient, we will feel His peace.

When Paul called me and told me he was giving up his practice and would be back in Houston in ten months, I was shocked. Because I love medicine so much, I hesitated to accept it. I asked, "But, Paul, are you sure you want to give that up? Are you sure you want to give up all that money, that favor, that beautiful home?"

Paul's response hit me like a ton of bricks. He said, "Mother, I'm not giving up; I'm gaining."

I will always remember that. Now I can see that he was listening to God instead of me, and I am so glad he did! Paul has been back working with the church since the latter part of 1999 and is a tremendous help not just to his younger brother, but to us all, providing oversight to the pastoral and discipleship ministries at Lakewood. God knew something that I didn't know. He also knew that by quitting his practice, plus helping people medically, Paul would have the freedom to travel all over the world to perform surgeries, fulfilling the calling He had given him when he was twelve years old.

JUST SAY YETH

My granddaughter Emily recently graduated from Texas A&M University. She has always been a happy little girl and somewhat feisty. When she was just a baby, she'd get so excited and she'd try to scream, "Yes!" when she just couldn't hold it in anymore. Instead, since she couldn't talk well yet, she would walk around the house yelling, "Yeth!" constantly.

This became a joke in our family, and after a while, I started using it when I encouraged the people at church. I'd say, "Wouldn't it be something if we all lived with that kind of enthusiasm? What if we walked around constantly saying, 'Yeth!' when God asked us to do something?"

We don't have to wait until we can say or do everything perfectly; He's just asking us to do it! Even if all you can say is "yeth," say it! Then do whatever it is He is asking of you. As Joel did, you might not have the confidence right away, but you can say, "Yeth," as you stand there in your Father's shoes. He is more than enough to get you through!

> We don't have to wait until we can say or do everything perfectly; God is just asking us to do it!

Life Lesson

God chooses ordinary people to do extraordinary things! But we must be willing, even when we don't feel we're quite ready for the challenge. What is God asking you to do? Do you feel inadequate? Always remember that you can stand in your heavenly Father's shoes. He promises to see you through, no matter how tough the task. If He has called you, He will equip you!

Chapter 21

God's Face Is Turned toward You

God is our refuge and strength, always ready to help in times of trouble.

Psalm 46:1 NLT

Settling into life without your spouse can be a hard thing to do. In my case, I had lived with John more than twice as long as I had lived without him! That's when I learned to truly rely on Deuteronomy 31:6, which states that God will never leave us nor forsake us. People will leave us, sometimes by choice, other times not by choice. But thank God, He is the one who is always constant in each of our lives.

There's just something that is so comforting about that, about knowing our Father is always watching out for us. When our oldest son, Paul, was young, his bedroom was down the hall from ours. When it was time to go to sleep, he would call out, "Daddy, are you there?"

John would respond, "Yes, Paul, I'm right here."

"Daddy, is your face turned toward me?"

I always thought that was so touching that our little boy would have been more frightened to think that John's face was turned away from him. It paints the perfect picture of our relationship with our heavenly Father. His face is always turned toward us, so we don't have to be afraid! When we trust in Him, He will direct our path. When we lean not to our own understanding, but acknowledge Him in all our ways, then He promises to lead us (Proverbs 3:5–6). I like God's ways a lot better than mine. He never makes a mistake, but I make plenty!

> Our heavenly Father's face is always turned toward us, so we don't have to be afraid!

I know without a doubt that God's face was turned toward me in 1981 when I was fighting cancer. I also felt it turned toward me after John's death in 1999. When he went to Heaven, it was like a part of all of us was gone, but God was watching. He led us and helped us make wise decisions. The right pieces began to fall into place, and the crooked places became straight. We found that not only is our Father always there to watch out for us, but He is also always there to hold us, to lift us up out of anything and everything trying to keep us down.

When my grandson Michael was little, he and his dad, Jim, went to the beach in Galveston, Texas. While they were out in the water, there was a sudden riptide that occurred, so Jim put Michael on his big six-foot-two-inch shoulders and told him not to let go. For minutes, Jim struggled to keep both of them from drowning. He tried to stick his toes in the sand to keep them from being swept away. He wasn't sure he was going to make it.

After a few minutes, little Michael looked at his dad and asked, "Daddy, are we going to die?"

Jim comforted Michael by assuring him that his daddy would take care of him. From that time on, Michael didn't say another word. Eventually they both made it to shore safely. What a frightening experience that must've been for a two-year-old! But once his daddy put him on his shoulders and told him he'd take care of him, Michael trusted him 100 percent.

That's how we feel when we are truly trusting in our heavenly Father. If we don't allow Him to pick us up, how will we stand when the tide comes?

In order to trust God's understanding and direction for our lives, we first must have full confidence that our God is a *good* God. Many times, especially in cases when our earthly father was not very supportive or loving, we feel as though our heavenly Father will not give us what's best, or even worse, that He will just flat out forget about us. Take it from someone who has experienced nearly seventy years of life with this Father—those thoughts couldn't be further from the truth!

I encourage you to trust God with your life. If you haven't yet met Jesus and don't yet know His love, this is a good time to get to know Him. He has been waiting for you!

"VICTORY DOES NOT ALWAYS COME OVERNIGHT"

My daughter Lisa and her husband, Kevin, tried for years to have a baby, but Lisa could not conceive. They both loved children and wanted at least three, and Kevin always hoped to have twins because he has a twin sister. After three years without success on their own, exploratory surgery showed that she had extensive endometriosis and scar tissue on her uterus, possibly a result from the mail bomb explosion.

Over the next three years, Lisa had two corrective surgeries and began the fertility process with an excellent fertility clinic— the hormones, injections, in vitro fertilization. Finally the doctor called them into his office and said, "Lisa, we've tried to help you, but enough is enough. We don't think we can do anything else to help you." He also gave her the name of a psychiatrist, knowing she would be dealing with a huge load of disappointment and heartache.

Walking out of that clinic in utter disbelief, the first thing

Kevin said to Lisa was, "Lisa, don't be discouraged, because our trust has never been in man, but in God."

Lisa knew that was true, but after this long, drawn-out medical process and devastating news, she was exhausted, emotionally and physically drained. She felt guilty that she was not able to give Kevin children and said she just felt trapped in a field of disappointment. She also began to have anxiety attacks, which totally took her by surprise.

She felt overwhelmed and had the thoughts we've all had at some point during our lives: *I've prayed and believed and done everything and endured everything I know to do, but nothing changed. What's wrong with me? Is all of this for nothing?*

We all face times of disappointment, confusion, and darkness when we don't understand why something didn't work out. The relationship ended, the promotion didn't come, one person receives healing and another person doesn't. I faced it with the cancer. God never promised that our lives would be trouble free. Sometimes we can't change our circumstance, but God can. We must get to the point where we trust God, even when we don't understand Him. By faith we take steps through the disappointment, knowing that He is good and will help us overcome.

Lisa and Kevin were determined to focus on the fact that God was not limited by their circumstances and that they would let God do what He would do and they would simply trust Him. During this time, they received a free sample of diapers in the mail one day—two diapers.

Kevin opened the package and declared, "Look, two diapers for our twins!"

That is faith talking! Kevin took a Sharpie pen and wrote on that package, "Our twins!" Then he tucked those diapers away as a promise from God.

Months later, Lisa received a call from Nancy Alcorn, the founder and president of Mercy Multiplied, which offers help to troubled girls, including those dealing with premarital pregnancies. Lisa and Nancy had both spoken at a conference a few years before, and our family and church connected with Nancy and supported her work.

Nancy wondered if Lisa and Kevin had any children yet, and when Lisa said not yet, Nancy continued to explain that a teenager was about to deliver twins and wanted to give up the babies for adoption to a loving Christian couple, but she had strict requirements, including that the couple have twins in their family. Would she and Kevin be interested in adopting the twins?

Nancy had no idea that Kevin had a twin sister! God not only answered the prayer of the young birth mother, but also fulfilled the dream of Kevin and Lisa's with one phone call! The God of miracles changed a mountain of disappointment in a divine appointment.

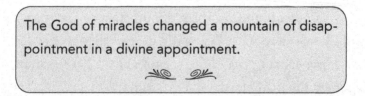

The God of miracles changed a mountain of disappointment in a divine appointment.

Even with the good news about the adoption, Lisa was still dealing with anxiety. She spent additional time reading and meditating on God's Word, and God began to restore her joy and brought her out of that horrible pit. During this time, John would take Lisa for walks to get her out of the house and to encourage her. One time she said to him, "Daddy, I prayed and read my Bible all morning, and I felt so good. But when I was finished, I felt bad again."

John said to her, "Lisa, victory doesn't always come overnight. You have to be consistent in doing the right thing, and you will break through with God's help."

Yes, it took several weeks, but the point is that God is faithful, whether it takes a little time or a lot of time. By the time the baby girls, Catherine and Caroline, arrived healthy and strong, Lisa was a happy mother and Kevin was an ecstatic father. Three years later, they adopted another child, Christopher. As Lisa would tell you today, God turned her "Why?" into a "Wow!" They are all teenagers today!

HIS GRACIOUS HAND IS UPON YOU

One of the stories I especially treasured during the months after John's death was the story of Nehemiah. When Nehemiah realized that the wall in his hometown of Jerusalem had been torn down, it deeply saddened him. In fact, it troubled him to the point of action. As the king of Persia's cupbearer,

Nehemiah asked for permission to speak to King Artaxerxes so that he could ask him for time to return home and rebuild the wall. In those days, that was a pretty big risk! But the Bible said that because the gracious hand of God was upon Nehemiah, the king granted him permission to speak.

When the king saw him, he immediately noticed his sorrow. He asked, "Why is your face sad when you are not sick?" Nehemiah explained that the wall in Jerusalem had been torn down and that he wanted to rebuild it. The king didn't even think twice, but gave him permission to go and rebuild it. So Nehemiah returned to Jerusalem, but soon after he started, two evil men, Sanballat and Tobiah, began to heckle and make threats to Nehemiah and his team. It got so bad that the men rebuilding the wall had to guard themselves as they worked.

The Bible says that they worked on the restoration of the walls with tools in one hand and a sword in the other. That sounds difficult, but it's necessary, even for us today. Some days we have to push through our work while having the sword of the Spirit, the Word of God, ready to combat our enemy. Nehemiah and his men ended up rebuilding the wall well and finishing it in record time. Nehemiah attributed all of his success to "the gracious hand of the Lord that was upon them."

Do you ever think about how the gracious hand of God has been on you throughout your life? You may have had adversities, but where would you be if God hadn't watched over you? I know that His hand has been on me since John has gone to Heaven. I sense His gracious hand every moment of every day, and I absolutely love it. I put my trust in His protection, and I am so thankful that His angels have charge over me to keep me in all my ways. Psalm 91 says He will do this for all of us if we choose to dwell in His secret place.

Life Lesson

We all face times of disappointment, confusion, and darkness when we don't understand why something didn't work out. God never promised that our lives would be trouble free. We must get to the point where we trust God, even when we don't understand Him. By faith we take steps through the disappointment, knowing God's face is always turned toward us, that He is good and will help us overcome.

Chapter 22
Who Are You Running For?

Let each of you look out not only for his own interests, but also for the interests of others.

Philippians 2:4

About twelve years ago, when Lakewood Church was still meeting in our old campus, a woman came to me and asked, "Dolores, do you remember me?" I was startled at first because no one besides my parents had called me Dolores since I was in high school. When I went to nursing school, the girls started calling me Dodie. I thought this woman looked familiar, but I couldn't quite remember who she was, so I asked her name. She said it was Joanne. Immediately I remembered her!

Joanne and I went to elementary school together. During

recess, when we would play baseball, she would serve as my pinch runner. I would hit the ball, and because I wore a brace and couldn't run fast, she would run the bases for me. When she reminded me of this, I began to cry. The remembrance that she cared enough about me to do that touched my heart. She was and still is so precious to me. I love Joanne and will always be thankful that I know her.

Driving home from church that day, I thought about how in life we should all be "running the bases" for one another. Of course, that most likely won't mean you're running literal bases for someone, as Joanne did for me. Still, there's always something you can do, say, or pray about for any person with whom you come in contact.

The Bible tells us to "carry each other's burdens, and in this way you will fulfill the law of Christ" (Galatians 6:2 NIV). Jesus is pleased with us when we look beyond our needs and see the needs of those around us and do something to help them. He is pleased when we "run the bases" for those who cannot run for themselves.

Since my conversation with Joanne, I have recounted several times when people have done this for me. My family, my church family, and my friends "ran the bases" for me in 1981 when I was diagnosed with metastatic cancer of the liver. They ran for me again when John was sick, and again when he went to be with Jesus. And the list goes on and on.

God doesn't want us to think only about ourselves in our own little worlds, distant from others and their needs. He wants us to become actively involved in one another's lives, to find a need and then help to meet it. That's one reason the Bible teaches us to get connected in a local church, so we can build relationships with people who will stand in for us when we need it, and so that we can do the same for them.

In the busyness of our day, it's easy to focus on getting done only what we need to do for ourselves. It seems we have enough on our own to-do list to keep us from even *thinking* about adding in anyone else's problems or responsibilities! When that happens to me, I remember Joanne. When she was running for me, she could've been focusing on saving her strength for her own at bat, but she didn't. She chose to run for me. I want to have the same heart for others!

Philippians 2:4 says, "Let each of you look out not only for his own interests, but also for the interests of others." God truly blesses those who look out for the welfare of those around them. There is no small life when it is given for the good of others!

When I do funerals, I often tell Joanne's story. I remind the people that we need to run the bases for the families of the deceased, because they are hurting and will be lonely. For these people to know that friends are praying for them helps them tremendously. I also remind them of the Bible story that recounts when Joshua and his army were fighting the Amale-kites (Exodus 17).

In that story, Moses took the rod of God up to the moun-taintop and held it up as the Israelites fought. As long as he held up his hands, Joshua was winning. After a while, Moses' arms got tired, just like we get tired and weary because of so much going on in our lives. But then Aaron and Hur intervened and propped Moses' arms up on some rocks and held his hands up—one on one side, one on the other—so that his hands remained steady till sunset, and Joshua won the battle. We all need our arms held up at times, even pastors and their families, just as our family has needed over the years. I am always so glad when people tell me they are praying for my family and for me.

As Bishop T. D. Jakes says, pastors' brains never stop, even when they are in bed trying to sleep. Their sermons, the church budget, the staff, the husband thinking about bills, the wife thinking about their schedule the next day—there are hundreds of things we are concerned about. And I'm sure you feel the same way in your busy schedule. But thank God we can *all* cast our cares on Him, because He cares for us. My husband cared for me dearly, but even he couldn't do what God can do!

START WHERE YOU ARE

Sometimes we think that because we are not a pastor or a speaker or someone with the ability to influence a huge audience of people at once, we are not capable of "running" for others and not important to the kingdom of God. That is so far from the truth! You never know what kind of impact you can have. To God, it makes no difference where you are or who you are. He can use you.

> You never know what kind of impact you can have. To God, it makes no difference where you are or who you are. He can use you.

I read a story about a schoolteacher named Mrs. Thompson who had taught fifth grade for years. She loved teaching and loved her students. But there was one student who was a problem to her. Ted didn't listen, wouldn't cooperate during recess, and came to school every day looking completely disheveled.

Mrs. Thompson thought she was being kind enough to him, but one day one of her other students challenged her. He asked, "Teacher, do you love us all the same?" She responded, "Of course I do." Then the child said, "Well, you don't act as though you love Ted." That hit Mrs. Thompson hard. She began to examine her heart. Was she judging him by his appearance and performance? Or was she seeing him for who God made him? Was she looking at his heart?

She decided then that she would do what she could to help the little boy, to show him that she cared. She began checking his records from previous grades. The records showed that Ted was an excellent student in first and second grade, but everything started to change when his mother died when he was in third grade. It seemed he hadn't been the same since. From that day on, Mrs. Thompson made up her mind that she was going to start teaching *students*, not just *school*. She began to show Ted a lot of attention and gave him extra help, and he slowly started to improve.

At Christmastime, Ted brought Mrs. Thompson a present wrapped in a paper bag. Inside were a bottle of used perfume and a rhinestone bracelet with some of the stones missing. She acted as though it was the best present she ever received. She had to fight back tears when Ted told her that these gifts had belonged to his mother, and again when he whispered, "You're the best teacher I ever had."

At that moment Mrs. Thompson realized that the love she showed Ted had made an impact on him. But it wasn't until years later that she truly realized how big that impact was. When Ted graduated from junior high, she got a letter from him informing her that he had graduated at the top of his class. When he graduated from high school, she received another letter saying the same thing. She was so proud.

Some years later, Mrs. Thompson received a letter letting her know that he had graduated from college. It was signed Ted Stoddard, M.D. She could hardly fight back the tears! Not long after that, a wedding invitation arrived with a special handwritten note asking Mrs. Thompson to come to the wedding and sit in the place of Ted's mother. She did, and when she went, she wore the rhinestone bracelet and the same kind of perfume he had given her years before. Ted thought she was beautiful and smelled just like his mother. How precious is that?

Mrs. Thompson "ran the bases" for Ted Stoddard, and it made a lasting impression on his life—one that likely totally changed the direction of his life and thousands of others who have been impacted by his life. The great news is that we can all have that kind of an impact. We just have to make a choice to show God's grace and love every day as the opportunity arises.

If you are a teacher or if you work with children, I salute you. You play such an important role in our society. You are shaping the next generation! I pray you fully understand the tremendous opportunity for influence that you have. I hope you see that like Mrs. Thompson, if you'll quit teaching school and start teaching children, you can make a lasting impact on your students' lives.

It really doesn't matter what your job is. We can all have great influence. Whether you're teaching a class of twenty children or speaking to twenty thousand people every week, God can use *you*. Whether you're in a business meeting, working in a refinery, in an office, in a hospital, *anywhere*—you are surrounded by opportunities to show God's love. Every person, every conversation, every situation is an opportunity.

If you don't know how to reach out to someone, ask Jesus to help make you aware of their needs.

As you start living a life of mercy, focused on the needs of others, you might find that people don't understand it, but they didn't understand Jesus either. All throughout the Bible, we see religious people condemning Him for spending time with the "sinners." He was despised for His unconditional love, and you might be too. But that's okay. Never let the opinions of others stop you from obeying Jesus. Part of our purpose on this earth is to grant grace to those who need it. Jesus will be so proud of us if we walk in love and are concerned about the needs of others, not just ourselves.

> Never let the opinions of others stop you from obeying Jesus.

DON'T LET SMALL STOP YOU

A few years ago, a precious lady moved to Houston and began attending Lakewood. Her mother had gone to Heaven four years before, and she felt she would never get over the pain of her loss. She walked into our church feeling depressed and overwhelmed, hoping to experience something in the service that would help her overcome the grief once and for all.

But to her surprise, the healing came before the service even began!

When this lady walked into the church, she was welcomed by one of our greeters. This time, however, the lady greeter felt impressed to greet this visitor in a far different manner than she would most guests. She walked up to this grieving lady, said hello, put her hands on her face, and patted it. Now, to you and me, that would probably seem odd. It is not the greeting you usually expect when you walk into church! You might just turn around and head for your car! But God knew just what that lady needed.

After the service, she came to me and said, "Ms. Dodie, how she put her hands on my face and patted it is exactly what my mother used to do to me. The lady didn't even know it!" From that day on, her grief began to leave her, and she has been living a different life ever since. And to think it all started with one woman's obedience to act, regardless of how small that act was. It started because of one woman's desire to look beyond herself and see someone else's needs.

It is amazing what God will lead us to do sometimes, if we will open up ourselves to Him and understand that no act is too small if He is in it. If we will listen to His still, small voice and obey it, we can make a great difference in the life of every person we come into contact with. Small acts can lead to great impacts. So don't let small stop you! The real way to win in this game of life is to run the bases for those who need it.

Life Lesson

You are surrounded by opportunities to show God's love. Every person, every conversation, every situation is an opportunity. If you will listen to God's still, small voice and obey it, you can make a great difference in the lives of other people. Small acts can lead to great impacts. The real way to win in this game of life is to run the bases for those who need it.

Chapter 23

Moments of Mercy

⸎

God blesses those who are merciful, for
they will be shown mercy.

Matthew 5:7 NLT

One of the main reasons we often refrain from reaching out
to others is because of our natural tendency to judge. It's part
of our human nature to judge people by their looks, circumstances, or experiences, paying little attention to their hearts.
But Jesus doesn't judge anyone by any of those things or by
their mistakes, so why should we? We are all called to be imitators of Him. Instead of constantly criticizing those around
us, we should serve as pictures of God's grace in their lives.

One of the best examples of this is the story of David in
the Bible (1 Samuel 16). Samuel, a seasoned prophet, was
instructed by God to anoint the next king of Israel. God sent

him to the home of Jesse, who lived in Bethlehem. Samuel told Jesse that one of his sons was to be anointed to take Saul's place as king. So Jesse called seven of his sons to stand before Samuel to find out which one it was.

As he met the prospects, Samuel thought about each one of Jesse's impressive sons, *He's tall and handsome. He speaks well and seems smart. Surely this is the one God has chosen!* But each time God replied with, "No, that's not him." Finally, they had gone through all seven candidates, and Samuel was confused as to what was wrong. So he asked Jesse, "Are these all the sons you have?"

Jesse replied, "There's still the youngest, but he's out tending the sheep."

Samuel asked for him to be brought in. As soon as David walked in the room, the Lord said to Samuel, "Rise and anoint him. This is the one!" Everyone was shocked! Little David, the one they thought wasn't even worth considering, the one who tended sheep and had killed a bear and a lion with his hands, was chosen by God to become the next king of Israel. And he grew up to be one of the greatest kings Israel has ever known, one of the greatest kings the world has ever known, a man after God's heart.

Later, when David volunteered to fight Goliath, his older brother Eliab burned with anger at him and asked what he was doing there. He said that he should be tending his few sheep. How sad that there was rivalry between the brothers! His own brothers couldn't see in David what God saw in him because they were looking only at the outward appearance.

The prophet Samuel learned a great lesson that day, a lesson we should all take to heart, which says, "The LORD does not look at the things people look at. People look at the outward appearance, but the LORD looks at the heart" (1 Samuel 16:7 NIV). We don't know people's hearts. We don't know their pasts or where they are coming from.

That's why we should always be people of mercy, extending love—not condemnation—to everyone we come into contact with. You never know who that person will become. You never know what they will accomplish for the kingdom of God. So don't ever pass someone up simply because you don't see their potential. Every day God makes beautiful what others look past as ordinary or lowly. I am so thankful for that!

A lot of times we get good at extending mercy to others in our own lives throughout the week, but it's a different story when we're at church. We want everyone to dress, talk, and act like a perfect Christian. But that's not what Jesus has in His heart for the church. As He said in His Word, it is not the healthy who need the doctor, but it is the sick (Mark 2:17).

I remember vividly a hot day in Houston. It was probably close to a hundred degrees as I was driving to church. I saw a lady walking down the sidewalk who was wearing a turtleneck shirt, which looked so out of place. I immediately thought, *What is wrong with that lady?* Then a sense of shame came on me, and I heard Jesus say in my heart, "How do you know she is not allergic to the sun or that she has a skin disease?" I repented!

My husband was so excellent at modeling Jesus' mercy. I always had a tremendous amount of respect for his love for people. John often said, "The church is not a museum to display perfect people, but a hospital for the hurting." It really is so true. Church should be a place free of judgment, always exuding the life-changing grace of God. It shouldn't be a place people want to avoid because they feel criticized or looked down upon. It should be the one place they know they will feel accepted and encouraged to live a better life. When we show love and when we are an imitator of the Lord Jesus, not condemning others, they will want to come to church. I always try to remember that if it wasn't for the grace of God, I could very well be the wounded and wayward one for whom no one cares.

Sometimes, when people treat us rudely, it is because they are going through something hard in their homes or lives. The Bible says that in the same way we judge others, we will be judged. When we are hard on others, we are setting ourselves up for trouble. Remember to make your words sweet, because you may have to eat them.

WHEN YOUR MERCY OUTLIVES YOU

One of my favorite stories in the Bible is found in Mark 14. Jesus had gone to the home of a man named "Simon the leper" to eat dinner. A woman heard that Jesus was there, so she went into the house with an alabaster jar filled with very expensive perfume. She broke the jar and poured the perfume on Jesus' head. Some of the guests attending the dinner saw this and were utterly disgusted by what she did. They rebuked her, telling her that she wasted the perfume. They said she should have sold it for a year's wages and given the money to the poor.

But Jesus defended the woman from the criticism. He said, "Leave her alone . . . She has done a beautiful thing to me. Truly I tell you, wherever the gospel is preached throughout the world, what she has done will also be told" (Mark 14:6–9). Isn't that amazing? From then on, anything that Jesus did, she had a role in!

That perfume was still on Jesus as He walked to the cross. The woman had poured it on Him for His darkest moment in life, so that He could make it to the brightest moment of His life, knowing that someone loved Him and had faith in Him. I'm sure that with every step He could still smell the fragrant oil.

As the fragrance mixed with the blood and sweat and fell from His head, Jesus probably thought back to that woman's act of mercy. While He carried the cross, He thought, *Somebody loves Me*. As He felt the nails tearing into His flesh, He thought, *Someone believes in Me*.

How beautiful would the world be if we all would strive to become that "someone" to the people in our lives? What would happen if we started pouring mercy on the crown of others when they're in the midst of their toughest times? I'll tell you what will happen: When they grow tired and feel hopeless, they will remember your act of kindness. They'll think, *I can make it. Someone loves me. Someone believes in me.* Your mercy can outlive you. Through it, you can accomplish more than you ever could have in one lifetime.

When John went through an unwanted divorce early in his pastoring, he was hurt and didn't know if he would ever preach again. But the people were wonderful to him, and they stood with him. He had so loved them and was so loved by them that they were merciful to him and stayed by his side.

On the seventy-fifth anniversary of that church, they invited John to come back and minister. When he spoke, he used that very story of the woman with the alabaster jar of perfume. He told those people the same thing that Jesus told that precious woman. He said that because they loved him, stood with him, and showed mercy to him, they were a part of everything he had done and was doing for Jesus. Whatever he did in life, every person whom he touched, they would have a part in it. John wept as he spoke, and so did everyone else who was there. It was one of his most beautiful and touching sermons. I was so proud of him.

In the same way, every good thing we do, whether a small act of kindness or a major investment of our time and effort, will outlive us. Anytime you extend grace to a friend, a family member, a coworker, or even someone you just met, you are linking yourself to their future. You are helping them become who God has created them to become.

It's like a domino effect. If you reach one person, who

reaches five others, who reaches ten others, who reaches a hundred others, your list starts to get pretty long! If you're tithing, serving in your church, or aiding people through missions, think about how large your reward will be. You now have a part in *every* soul who is reached through your church.

You may not get the same recognition from people as the pastor or the missionary or the teacher, but always remember that Jesus sees the work you're doing. You are "staying by the stuff," as John would say, and you will be rewarded. Always remember what Jesus said: "Inasmuch as you did *it* to one of the least of these My brethren, you did *it* to Me" (Matthew 25:40).

DON'T PASS UP A MOMENT FOR MERCY

When you start to see life in this way, as an opportunity to affect others so that your mercy outlives you, you begin to seize every moment. You start to take more advantage of your time, knowing that there are going to be many people on the other side of your mercy.

I remember one day my eyes were opened to this truth. I was driving down a busy street on my way home when I saw one of the ladies from our church standing at the bus stop with groceries in her arms. I remembered that she had scoliosis and had recently gone through a divorce. She still had children living at home, including a special-needs child. I felt such compassion for her.

As soon as I passed her, the Lord spoke to my heart to go back, pick her up, and give her a ride to her house. I didn't need to rush home for any reason, but I just wasn't in the mood to detour.

The farther I drove, the more miserable I got. I knew I was being selfish, but I didn't want to get off schedule! Finally, my conscience won the battle, and I turned around and went back to pick the lady up. She was so overjoyed that I would do this. I drove her to her house, let her out, and continued on my way home, still a little disgruntled because I had been delayed. Sure, I listened, but I didn't have a cheerful attitude. I was not showing mercy the way Jesus did. I was complaining!

Over the years, I forgot about the incident. But one day about fifteen years later, after they moved to a different city I got a call from the woman's daughter. She said, "Ms. Dodie, my mother has gone on to Heaven, but I want you to know that she never stopped talking about the day you stopped and drove her home with those groceries." She then asked me to pray for her, as she would assume the responsibility of caring for her special-needs brother who was in his twenties by then.

I was deeply touched and humbled. It was a strong reminder to not just do what God says, but to do it with a willing heart. Jesus never complained when He was asked to show mercy. Not even in the greatest act of mercy—dying on the cross for us! So why should we complain about helping others? What we do today can touch a person's life not just now, but it can continue to touch them and those connected to them for years to come. That's why we should never, ever, *ever* pass up a moment to show mercy.

May I remind you that Jesus loves you with an everlasting love, and so do I. No matter what you have done in life, God's love for you will never change.

Be encouraged! You are someone special and God has something special for you to do.

Run the bases for others, and it will please Jesus! Be your best for Him and an imitator of Him. I love you!

Life Lesson

Anytime you extend grace to a friend, a family member, a coworker, or even someone you just met, you are linking yourself to their future and helping them become who God has created them to become. That's why we should never, ever, *ever* pass up a moment to show mercy, whether it is a small act of kindness or a major investment of our time and effort. Your mercy can outlive you.

Conclusion

I was devastated in 1981 when I was diagnosed with metastatic cancer of the liver and given a few weeks to live. It was right at Christmastime, and it was a very sad time for my family. On the morning of December 11, 1981, the day after I went home from the hospital, John and I lay facedown in our bedroom and prayed, and I knew that I was healed. It didn't feel like it, and the symptoms did not leave immediately, but I accepted in my heart that beyond a shadow of a doubt it was done. As I continued to trust Jesus, read His Word and confessed His healing scriptures, prayed for the sick, and asked others to forgive me, my healing came. I would never want you to go through what I went through, but if you do, God will give you help and courage.

All of us have difficulties at times in our lives, and it seems hard to go on. Whatever you are dealing with, remember that nothing is too difficult for God. Jesus hasn't changed and He never will change. He walked the shores of the Sea of Galilee and healed all who came to Him, and He still does it today. He loves you with an everlasting love and has a way through the illness or the financial setback, through the heartbreak— through *everything*. He will help you overcome the disappointments you have, or the pain caused by people you thought were your friends or those closest to you. The good thing about it is that you can talk to Him anytime, because He is always awake!

There is hope and a future for you because Jesus is hope. You are of such great value to God that He sent His Son Jesus to die on the cross for you. He has His hand upon you for good, to give you a future and hope. You may have gone through some hurdles, but He will help you win the race— perhaps not in the way you think, but in His way, and God's way is always the best way. So don't give up, seek Him, and serve Him with all your heart. He is waiting for you to move. Remember that it is not how you started your life but how you finish that matters, and He can take you so much further than you ever dreamed possible.

Remember that our God is the God of a million second chances. No matter where you come from, no matter how low-down you have been, no matter what you've done in life, Jesus still loves you, forgives you, and never ever gives up on you. Isaiah 43:25 says, "I, even I, am the one who wipes out your transgressions for My own sake, and I will not remember your sins" (NASB). We remember our sins, but God deletes our sins and removes them as far as the east is from the west. If you keep bringing up your sins, He will ask you, "What sins?"

I think the best advice I can give you is to be an imitator of Jesus. Have Him living in your heart, know what His Word says, and love and be kind to people. That's what Jesus did. He walked in love, didn't judge, encouraged the brokenhearted and healed the sick and bruised. Love as Jesus did. Care for others. Pray for others. Just be like Jesus.

Appendix 1
The Plan of Salvation

1. *We are all sinners.* "For all have sinned and fall short of the glory of God" (Romans 3:23).

2. *Jesus died for our sins.* "God demonstrates His own love toward us, in that while we were still sinners, Christ died for us" (Romans 5:8).

3. *God loves you unconditionally.* "For God so loved the world that He gave His only begotten Son, that whoever believes in Him should not perish but have everlasting life" (John 3:16).

4. *Jesus will give you eternal life.* "For the wages of sin *is* death, but the gift of God *is* eternal life in Christ Jesus our Lord" (Romans 6:23).

5. *You will become a child of God.* "But as many as received Him, to them He gave the right to become children of God, to those who believe in His name" (John 1:12).

6. *You must believe Jesus is your Lord and Savior, and you will be saved.* "If you confess with your mouth the Lord Jesus and believe in your heart that God has raised Him from the dead, you will be saved. For with the heart one believes unto righteousness, and with the mouth confession is made unto salvation" (Romans 10:9–10).

SALVATION PRAYER

Dear God, I admit that I am a sinner and I am in need of a Savior. I repent of my sins and ask You to forgive me. Jesus, I ask You to come into my life and be my Lord and Savior. I receive Your forgiveness, and I want to serve You all the days of my life. Teach me Your ways that I may walk in Your will. Amen.

_____   _____

Name   Date

If you just prayed this prayer, congratulations! You have just made the single greatest decision of your life. I am so proud of you! Now, not only will you spend an eternity with Jesus in Heaven, but you have also opened yourself up to His wonderful leading while on the earth. And God is always faithful to His children!

Appendix 2
Scriptural Confessions

Speak what God says about you. Boldly make this confession:

I know who I am in Christ!

I know what I can do in Christ!

I bear the name of Jesus!

I am washed by the blood of Jesus!

I am in the family of God!

I have the life of God in me!

I am filled with the Spirit of God!

I am in the kingdom of God!

I resist the devil and he flees from me!

Make these declarations about yourself:

I am of God (1 John 4:4).

I have overcome the evil one (1 John 4:4).

Greater is He that is in me than he that is in the world (1 John 4:4).

Christ has redeemed me from the curse of the law (Galatians 3:13).

I am living in the blessings of Abraham (Galatians 3:14).

I am blessed in the city. I am blessed in the field (Deuteronomy 28:3).

I am blessed when I go out. I am blessed when I come in (Deuteronomy 28:6).

I know who I am in Christ. I bear the name of Jesus. Satan will not steal one thing that God has given me (John 10:10).

I am strong in the Lord and the power of His might (Ephesians 6:10).

I have on the whole armor of God (Ephesians 6:11).

I am able to stand against all the wiles and all the strategies of the enemy (Ephesians 6:11).

I stand my ground. Having done all, I stand (Ephesians 6:13).

I am more than a conqueror (Romans 8:37).

I will not be ashamed of Jesus or His Word (Romans 1:16).

I will stand tall as a child of God (see 2 Chronicles 20:17).

I will bear the name that is above every name, the name of Jesus (Philippians 2:9–10).

I will drive the enemy from the field of battle (James 4:7).

Healing is mine (1 Peter 2:24).

Wholeness is mine (3 John 2).

All my needs have been supplied. I will begin to act like it (Philippians 4:19).

God's blessings are mine (Galatians 3:14).

Appendix 3
Healing Scriptures

One of the most important things that helped me to be healed was the unshakable confidence I had in the Word of God. What follows is a list of scriptures that helped me most. I still read them every day to build and sustain my faith.

Daily reading and meditating on these healing promises was one of the major keys to my healing because it helped me focus on what God said about me and not how I felt. I believe they will help you in your battle to overcome every symptom and every lie of the enemy.

> "If you diligently heed the voice of the Lord your God and do what is right in His sight, give ear to His commandments and keep all His statutes, I will put none of the diseases on you which I have brought on the Egyptians. For I *am* the Lord who heals you."
>
> Exodus 15:26

> "So you shall serve the Lord your God, and He will bless your bread and your

water. And I will take sickness away from the midst of you. No one shall suffer miscarriage or be barren in your land; I will fulfill the number of your days."

Exodus 23:25–26

"And the LORD will take away from you all sickness, and will afflict you with none of the terrible diseases of Egypt which you have known, but will lay *them* on all those who hate you."

Deuteronomy 7:15

"Now it shall come to pass, if you diligently obey the voice of the LORD your God, to observe carefully all His commandments which I command you today, that the LORD your God will set you high above all nations of the earth. And all these blessings shall come upon you and overtake you, because you obey the voice of the LORD your God."

Deuteronomy 28:1–2

"I call heaven and earth as witnesses today against you, *that* I have set before you life and death, blessing and cursing; therefore choose life, that both you and your descendants may live; that you may love the LORD your God, that you may obey His voice, and that you may cling to Him, for He *is* your life and the length of your days."

Deuteronomy 30:19–20

Not a word failed of any good thing which the LORD had spoken to the house of Israel. All came to pass.

Joshua 21:45

"There has not failed one word of all His good promise, which He promised through His servant Moses."

1 Kings 8:56

"My covenant I will not break, nor alter the word that has gone out of My lips."

Psalm 89:34

No evil shall befall you, nor shall any plague come near your dwelling; for He shall give His angels charge over you, to keep you in all your ways. ". . . He shall call upon Me, and I will answer him; I *will* be with him in trouble; I will deliver him and honor him. With long life I will satisfy him, and show him My salvation."

Psalm 91:10–11, 15–16

Who heals all your diseases.

Psalm 103:3

He also brought them out with silver and gold, and *there* was none feeble among His tribes.

Psalm 105:37

He sent His word and healed them, and delivered *them* from their destructions.

Psalm 107:20

I shall not die, but live, and declare the works of the LORD.

Psalm 118:17

Trust in the LORD with all your heart, and lean not on your own understanding; in all your ways acknowledge Him, and He shall direct your paths. Do not be wise in your own eyes; fear the LORD and depart from evil. It will be health to your flesh, and strength to your bones.

Proverbs 3:5–8

My son, give attention to my words; incline your ear to my sayings. Do not let them depart from your eyes; keep them in the midst of your heart; for they *are* life to those who find them, and health to all their flesh.

Proverbs 4:20–22

" 'Fear not, for I *am* with you; be not dismayed, for I *am* your God. I will strengthen you, yes, I will help you, I will uphold you with My righteous right hand.' "

Isaiah 41:10

"For I, the Lord your God, will hold your right hand, saying to you, 'Fear not, I will help you.' "

Isaiah 41:13

"I, *even* I, *am* He who blots out your transgressions for My own sake; and I will not remember your sins. Put Me in remembrance; let us contend together; state *your* case, that you may be acquitted."

Isaiah 43:25–26

But He *was* wounded for our transgressions, *He was* bruised for our iniquities; the chastisement for our peace *was* upon Him, and by His stripes we are healed.

Isaiah 53:5

Then the Lord said to me, "You have seen well, for I am ready to perform My word."

Jeremiah 1:12

" 'For I will restore health to you and heal you of your wounds,' says the Lord."

Jeremiah 30:17

"My people are destroyed for lack of knowledge."

Hosea 4:6

"Let the weak say, 'I am strong.' "

Joel 3:10

The Lord *is* good, a stronghold in the day of trouble; and He knows those who trust in Him.

Nahum 1:7

He will make an utter end of *it*. Affliction will not rise up a second time.

Nahum 1:9

"Bring all the tithes into the storehouse, that there may be food in My house, and try Me now in this," says the Lord of hosts, "if I will not open for you the windows of heaven and pour out for you *such* blessing that *there will* not *be room* enough *to receive it.*"

Malachi 3:10

And behold, a leper came and worshiped Him, saying, "Lord, if You are willing, You can make me clean." Then Jesus put out *His* hand and touched him, saying, "I am willing; be cleansed." Immediately his leprosy was cleansed.

Matthew 8:2–3

"He Himself took our infirmities and bore our sicknesses."

Matthew 8:17

"Whatever you bind on earth will be bound in heaven, and whatever you loose on earth will be loosed in heaven."

Matthew 18:18

"If two of you agree on earth concerning anything that they ask, it will be done for them by My Father in heaven. For where two or three are gathered together in My name, I am there in the midst of them."

Matthew 18:19–20

"If you have faith and do not doubt, you will not only do what was done to the fig tree, but also if you say to this mountain, 'Be removed and be cast into the sea,' it will be done. And whatever things you ask in prayer, believing, you will receive."

Matthew 21:21–22

"Have faith in God. For assuredly, I say to you, whoever says to this mountain, 'Be removed and be cast into the sea,' and does not doubt in his heart, but believes that those things he says will be done, he will have whatever he says. Therefore I say to you, whatever things you ask when you pray, believe that you receive *them*, and you will have *them*."

Mark 11:22–24

"And these signs will follow those who believe: In My name they will cast out demons; they will speak with new tongues; they will take up serpents; and if they drink anything deadly, it will by no means hurt them; they will lay hands on the sick, and they will recover."

Mark 16:17–18

"Behold, I give you the authority to trample on serpents and scorpions, and over all the power of the enemy, and nothing shall by any means hurt you."

Luke 10:19

"Now we know that God does not hear sinners; but if anyone is a worshiper of God and does His will, He hears him."

John 9:31

"The thief does not come except to steal, and to kill, and to destroy. I have come that they may have life, and that they may have *it* more abundantly."

John 10:10

And not being weak in faith, he did not consider his own body, already dead (since he was about a hundred years old), and the deadness of Sarah's womb. He did not waver at the promise of God through unbelief, but was strengthened in faith, giving glory to God, and being fully convinced that what He had promised He was also able to perform.

Romans 4:19–21

But if the Spirit of Him who raised Jesus from the dead dwells in you, He who raised Christ from the dead will also give life to your mortal bodies through His Spirit who dwells in you.

Romans 8:11

For the weapons of our warfare *are* not carnal but mighty in God for pulling down strongholds, casting down arguments and every high thing that exalts itself against the knowledge of God, bringing every thought into captivity to the obedience of Christ.

2 Corinthians 10:4—5

Christ has redeemed us from the curse of the law.

Galatians 3:13

Finally, my brethren, be strong in the Lord and in the power of His might. Put on the whole armor of God, that you may be able to stand against the wiles of the devil. For we do not wrestle against flesh and blood, but against principalities, against powers, against the rulers of the darkness of this age, against spiritual *hosts* of wickedness in the heavenly *places*. Therefore take up the whole armor of God, that you may be able to withstand in the evil day, and having done all, to stand.

Stand therefore, having girded your waist with truth, having put on the breastplate of righteousness, and having shod your feet with the preparation of the gospel of peace; above all, taking the shield of faith with which you will be able to quench all the fiery darts of the wicked one. And take the helmet of salvation, and the sword of the Spirit, which is the word of God.

Ephesians 6:10–17

He who has begun a good work in you will complete *it* until the day of Jesus Christ.

Philippians 1:6

For it is God who works in you both to will and to do for *His* good pleasure.

Philippians 2:13

Be anxious for nothing, but in everything by prayer and supplication, with thanksgiving, let your requests be made known to God; and the peace of God, which surpasses all understanding, will guard your hearts and minds through Christ Jesus. Finally, brethren, whatever things are true, whatever things *are* noble, whatever things *are* just, whatever things *are* pure, whatever things *are* lovely, whatever things *are* of good report, if *there is* any virtue and if *there is* anything praiseworthy—meditate on these things.

Philippians 4:6–8

For God has not given us a spirit of fear, but of power and of love and of a sound mind.

2 Timothy 1:7

For the word of God *is* living and powerful, and sharper than any two-edged sword, piercing even to the division of soul and spirit, and of joints and marrow, and is a discerner of the thoughts and intents of the heart.

Hebrews 4:12

Let us hold fast the confession of *our* hope without wavering, for He who promised *is* faithful.

Hebrews 10:23

Not forsaking the assembling of ourselves together, as *is* the manner of some, but exhorting *one another*, and so much the more as you see the Day approaching.

Hebrews 10:25

Therefore do not cast away your confidence, which has great reward.

Hebrews 10:35

By faith Sarah herself also received strength to conceive seed, and she bore a child when she was past the age, because she judged Him faithful who had promised.

Hebrews 11:11

Jesus Christ *is* the same yesterday, today, and forever.

Hebrews 13:8

If any of you lacks wisdom, let him ask of God, who gives to all liberally and without reproach, and it will be given to him.

James 1:5

But the wisdom that is from above is first pure, then peaceable, gentle, willing to yield, full of mercy and good fruits, without partiality and without hypocrisy.

James 3:17

Therefore submit to God. Resist the devil and he will flee from you. Draw near to God and He will draw near to you.

Cleanse *your* hands, *you* sinners; and purify *your* hearts.

James 4:7–8

Is anyone among you sick? Let him call for the elders of the church, and let them pray over him, anointing him with oil in the name of the Lord. And the prayer of faith will save the sick, and the Lord will raise him up.

James 5:14–15

But you *are* a chosen generation, a royal priesthood, a holy nation, His own special people, that you may proclaim the praises of Him who called you out of darkness into His marvelous light.

1 Peter 2:9

Who Himself bore our sins in His own body on the tree, that we, having died to sins, might live for righteousness—by whose stripes you were healed.

1 Peter 2:24

Casting all your care upon Him, for He cares for you. Be sober, be vigilant; because your adversary the devil walks about like a roaring lion, seeking whom he may devour. Resist him, steadfast in the faith, knowing that the same sufferings are experienced by your brotherhood in the world.

1 Peter 5:7–9

Beloved, if our heart does not condemn us, we have confidence toward God. And whatever we ask we receive from Him, because we keep His commandments and do those things that are pleasing in His sight.

1 John 3:21–22

Now this is the confidence that we have in Him, that if we ask anything according to His will, He hears us. And if we know that He hears us, whatever we ask, we know that we have the petitions that we have asked of Him.

1 John 5:14–15

Beloved, I pray that you may prosper in all things and be in health, just as your soul prospers.

3 John 1:2

And they overcame him by the blood of the Lamb and by the word of their testimony, and they did not love their lives to the death.

Revelation 12:11

Acknowledgments

When my beloved husband, John, passed away, God spoke to me to write a book and He even gave me the title. It's been in my heart for almost seventeen years now, and it has finally come into fruition. Sometimes when we have a desire it doesn't happen overnight. I have so many people to thank for helping me see my dream come to pass.

I offer special thanks to Andrea Graff, my precious granddaughter, for her invaluable work on this project from the very beginning. I was thrilled to work with her!

I am grateful for my daughter Lisa, who encouraged me to write this book that God put in my heart to do. She managed this project from start to finish, and I appreciate her labor of love.

I want to thank my publisher, Rolf Zettersten, at Faith-Words/Hachette Book Group and his wonderful team, Joey Paul and Becky Hughes, for believing in me and my family.

I am grateful also to my literary agents, Jan Miller Rich and Shannon Marven, at Dupree Miller & Associates for their guidance and support throughout the entire process.

I appreciate Jeanette Thomason for all her contributions,

and Lance Wubbels for his wisdom and wordsmithing to help keep my message clear.

I deeply appreciate and love the wonderful members of Lakewood Church who have stood with me, shared in many of the stories of this book, and touched my life in so many ways, as well as those around the world who have faithfully supported our ministry over these many years. You are all part of our Lakewood family.

And last but not least, thanks to our beautiful children, Paul, Lisa, Tamara, Joel, and April. You are remarkable and I am so proud of each of you. I love you.

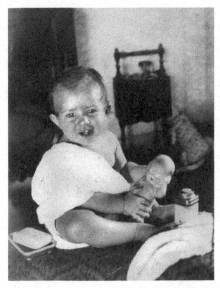

Dolores Ann Pilgrim is what my parents named me. Eventually *Dodie* was the nickname that stuck.

My mother standing on the porch of our new home, which I grew up in.

Here I am with my dad at age five. As a result of polio, I wore the brace you see on my right leg until I was in the fourth grade.

I was thirteen when I accepted Jesus into my heart. It was the best decision I have ever made.

I was in the color guard in the Lee Brigadiers corps at my high school.

After high school, I attended the Lillie Jolly School of Nursing, where I realized that taking care of sick people was one of my greatest passions.

John was seventeen when he accepted Jesus Christ as his Savior.

My parents, Georgia and Roy Pilgrim, in 1928. What a stylish couple!

My parents in their eighties. They set an excellent example for me and my children.

Everything about our wedding day in 1954 was perfect.

Our daughter Lisa at six months. Her healing inspired John to change the course of his ministry and life.

John and me in 1981, just a few months before I was diagnosed with cancer.

My five precious children in 1966 (from the top clockwise)—Paul, Tamara, April, Joel, and Lisa.

Children grow up so fast. Here are pictures of Paul, Lisa, Tamara, Joel, and April in elementary school alongside a recent photo.

Paul

Lisa

Tamara

Joel

April

The infamous Gray Box was one of the ways John taught our children about God's faithfulness in meeting our needs.

Here is Joel with our dog Scooter, who taught us what *not* to do when adversity comes barking.

On Mother's Day 1959, John and I founded Lakewood Church in an abandoned feed store.

In the 1970s, God helped us build a sanctuary seating 1,000 people, which we eventually expanded to seat 5,000.

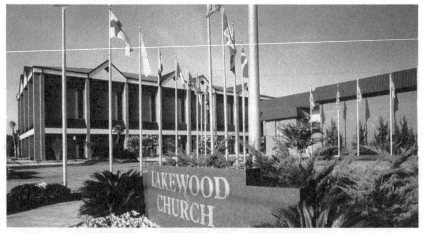

In 1987, God blessed us with an 8,000-seat sanctuary built debt free.

NEW JOBS, NEW DIAL FOR OILERS — IN SPORTS DAY/C-1

The Houston Post

On January 30, 1990, God performed a miracle when Lisa survived a package bomb that literally exploded in her lap.

Package bomb rocks city church

The guiding force of Lakewood Church

Lisa and Kevin's three miracle children in 2001—twins Catherine and Caroline with their new baby brother, Christopher.

John hosted the weekly *John Osteen* television program for sixteen years, reaching millions in the U.S. and around the world.

Here we are cutting the cake at our fortieth wedding anniversary dinner, which the children surprised us with.

John and I were a team in every sense of that word.

After John's death in 1999, my youngest son, Joel, succeeded him as pastor of Lakewood Church.

It's 2004 and Joel and I are standing in front of some of the Compaq Center renovation work.

Here I am with Joel, his wife, Victoria, and their two children, Alexandra and Jonathan, at the 2005 grand opening of the current Lakewood Church.

Lakewood Church today sits alongside U.S. Highway 59, close to downtown Houston, Texas.

Lakewood Church seats 16,000 with over 45,000 in attendance at five weekly services, as well as two Spanish services.

Today, after having Joel as pastor of Lakewood Church for seventeen years, it's hard to remember that he had never preached a message in his life until the last Sunday before John's death.

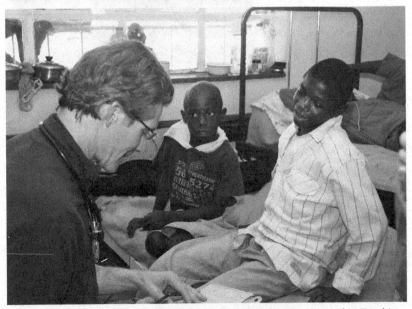

Paul is making the rounds with the patients in Mukinge Mission Hospital in Zambia.

Since John's passing, I've stayed busy sharing my testimony and praying for the sick.

One of the great joys of my life is praying for the needs of people.

I love praying for children and often have prayer services for special needs children.

In 1999, I threw the opening pitch at a Houston Astros baseball game. No one thought I could even throw a ball at age sixty-six, but I got it all the way to home plate.

I share my personal testimony at the Night of Hope events, something I have done for ten years now.

Lisa, Paul, and I were honored to meet with Billy Graham in 2007.

Here I am in 2001 on Thanksgiving Day with my then eighteen grandchildren (one grandson yet to come). I now also have one great-granddaughter.

A recent family photo of Joel, Lisa, April, me, Tamara, and Paul. I am so proud of each of them, their mates, and their families. They are all serving in the full-time ministry.

LSC NC 12.22.2022 #